THE
EFFECTIVE
MANAGER

MARK HORSTMAN

Cofounder, Manager Tools

Published by John Wiley & Sons, Inc., Hoboken, New Jersey.
Published simultaneously in Canada.

For general information on our other products and services or for technical support, please contact our Customer Care Department within the United States at (800) 762-2974, outside the United States at (317) 572-3993 or fax (317) 572-4002.

Wiley also publishes its books in a variety of electronic formats. Some content that appears in print may not be available in electronic books. For more information about Wiley products, visit our web site at www.wiley.com.

ISBN 978-1-119-24460-8 (cloth); ISBN 978-1-119-28611-0 (ePDF);
ISBN 978-1-119-28612-7 (ePub)

Printed in the United States of America

SKY10035896_090622

This is what I tell my friends

Dedicated to my wife Rhonda and our wonderful children:
Kate, Travis, Ashley, Courtney, Drake, Christopher, and Jaggars

On behalf of Mike Auzenne, my Manager Tools cofounder
and our great team of professionals at Manager Tools

Contents

Introduction

Who This Book Is for,
What It's about, and Why

IF YOU'RE A MANAGER, this book was written for you. If you've ever struggled to lead your team or wondered how to handle a difficult situation, this book is for you. If you find the people side of management (and that's all this book is about) difficult at times, this book is *definitely* for you.

To be clear: this book isn't about "management" the way most business publications talk about it. To them, "management" means big organizational ideas like strategy, or finance, or organizational change. If you scan the Management section of *The Wall Street Journal*, you'll see articles about those topics. That's not what this book is about. Frankly, if you're just a frontline manager, or maybe even a director, you don't need to know a lot about that kind of "management" just yet. What you do need to know about is how to manage people. If that's you, this book is for you.

This book is about managing people. It's about getting the most out of your direct reports, for two reasons: *because most managers are very bad at that part of their job,* **yet that's the most valuable thing they do as a manager.**

Isn't that sad? Most managers are terrible at the most important thing they're supposed to be doing: getting top performances out of the people they are managing.

In a way, though, it's not surprising. Lots of folks think getting a Master of Business Administration (MBA) will make them managers. But MBA programs don't teach much about managing people. Part of the reason for that is that many of the professors have never managed a group of people with responsibility for their output. Also, people aren't easily placed into neat concep-tualized models that can be analyzed and measured. People are messy.

Hundreds, if not thousands, of managers describe their "training" this way: *I got promoted, and they didn't tell me anything about what I was supposed to do or how I was supposed to do it. They just gave me a team and wished me luck.*

One new manager I worked with, years ago at a great firm, told me that the day he got promoted, his new boss handed him a stack of folders regarding his team members, pointed to a corner of the building, and said, "Your team sits over there, by the windows."

This is mind-boggling. The upside of this, however, is that *you're not alone.* That feeling you have that others know what they're doing but you don't is wrong. *Almost everyone else doesn't know either.*

So, give yourself a break. Let yourself off the hook. You're doing a difficult job, and you haven't been given ample preparation. That's why I wrote *The Effective Manager.*

The Effective Manager will only concern itself with actionable guidance. Usually, I will not tell you "how to be" or "what to reflect on" or "what attitude to have." There's a part of me, after 25 years of coaching managers, that doesn't really care what kind of attitude you have, because all the attitude in the world isn't going to change the results. The only thing that will change the results is to change what you DO.

Several years ago, a senior vice president asked me to coach one of his key team members, Paul. He said that his direct (someone who reported directly to him), who was a vice president, was brilliant and had almost everything it took to be a more senior manager. The problem was that he was a horrible presenter when compared with his peers, and he would never make it to higher levels because he would have to give presentations regularly. In addition, he was a nervous presenter, and it was excruciating to be in the audience when he talked.

I asked Paul to present something for me. Yes, he was extremely nervous. There was no way Paul would be going further in his career. I still remember being amazed that he had gotten as far as he had. (His boss had sheltered him, and, frankly, it was probably a good move, as bad off as Paul was.)

I suppose I could have engaged a hypnotist, or I could have impersonated a therapist and tried to "understand" Paul's emotional state. But, really, I didn't care very much how nervous Paul was. What I cared about was what he *did* that made the audience think he was nervous. If I could help him eliminate all the behaviors that audiences judged as "nervous," he would be fine.

This probably surprises you a little. But let's do a little thought experiment. Suppose that Paul got up in front of the senior team the following week and presented brilliantly. There were no mistakes, no long embarrassing pauses, no stammering, no "deer in the head-lights" moments, and not a single "ummm" or "ahhhhh . . ."

Paul's boss would surely think, "Success!" He might even say to Paul, "You beat it! You weren't nervous!"

But I can tell you what Paul would say: "No way. I was so nervous; I nearly threw up right before my presentation."

Do you understand? An audience doesn't react to a speaker's nervousness. They react *to the behaviors that they see and hear that they ascribe to nerves.* If Paul is nervous but doesn't behave as if he is nervous, will his audience notice? Of course not. They'll think he's confident.

Suppose Paul is *not* nervous, but he engages in all the behaviors that a nervous person engages in. What is the audience going to think? That he's nervous and not confident. At the executive level, that's the kiss of death.

Success at work is about what you *do*—you are your behaviors. Almost nothing else matters. And that's what *The Effective Manager* is about.

About Manager Tools

My firm, which I co-own with my outstanding business partner Michael Auzenne, is a management consultant firm. We coach managers and executives at firms all around the world. We train managers at firms all over the world. In 2016, we will provide all-day training sessions to over 10,000 managers at our corporate clients worldwide. We also host training conferences all over the world, where individual managers can get trained. We will conduct over 100 of these training conferences in 2016.

However, if your company cannot afford to send you to training (we do offer a discount if you want to pay yourself), *every bit of guidance in this book is available for free in our podcast, Manager Tools.* You can find the podcast on iTunes and at www.manager-tools.com.

As of this writing, our podcasts are downloaded about a million times a month, in virtually every country in the world. We've won many Podcast Awards over the years, thanks to our loyal audience.

Our podcast is free because the mission of our firm is to make every manager in the world effective, and many of them can't afford to buy this book.

Periodically, I will encourage you to go to our website for more guidance. I can't put all the podcasts in here—there are, at the time of this publishing, close to 1,000 of them. You'll see many instances of There's a Cast for That™ throughout this book. There are links to additional free content in our podcasts on our website.

I encourage you to visit www.manager-tools.com and learn even more. Click on the "There's a Cast for That™" link near the top right of our home page for a full listing of all of the podcasts cited in the *The Effective Manager*.

A Note about Data

For the past 25 years, we've been testing various managerial behaviors and tools to see which work and which don't. I used to hate it when the manager training I received, or the books I read, basically were filled with someone's opinions, or they proffered an idea and then used a few anecdotes to support the person's position. We at Manager Tools like the aphorism, "The plural of anecdote is not data."

We have tested and refined all of the four primary recommendations given in this book. We have tested or surveyed over 91,000 managers at various times, for various behaviors, responses, and outcomes.

In many tests, we track results and retention of managers in both a test group and an unchanged control group. This is especially true of the Four Most Effective Behaviors. We have also tested many of the *phrases* that we recommend you use. Our tests show a slight difference in responses, for instance, when using the phrases, "Would you please . . . ?" and "Would you . . . ?" We recommend using "Would you please . . . ?"

That being said, no survey can completely predict how any one manager's results, retention, or relationships will be affected by the tools we recommend. Every situation is different. Often, that's what many managers say when they come to us for help and explain their situation: "My situation is special/different/unique." Almost always, it's not different at all. But because there's a chance that a manager's situation *is* unique, we will tell you this: *Our guidance is for 90 percent of managers, 90 percent of the time.* It's possible that you're in a special situation, but I doubt it.

A Note about Gender

You'll notice that, throughout this book, I'll use different genders for managers—sometimes male and sometimes female. All of our content at Manager Tools—all of the audio guidance in podcasts and all the "show notes"—use a nearly perfect balance of male and female examples. (If you're a male, and it seems as if there are a lot of female examples, that says more about your biases than our examples.)

The reason for using different genders for managers throughout this book is that all of our data show that men and women make equally good managers and, for that matter, executives. If you're a female manager, we're glad you're reading this book, and we're here to help.

Now, let's find out what it takes to be a good manager and *how to do it.*

1

What Is an Effective Manager?

THERE'S A LOT OF TALK about what good management is. When someone tells you they know how to manage or what it takes to manage, ask them, "How do you measure what a good manager is, or does?" If you don't get a crisp answer (like the one I outline below), don't take what they tell you very seriously.

I suspect you've known both good and bad managers. What makes them so? Is it what they do? How they think? Their personality? What they feel? Where they went to school?

Think about this for a minute: *How do you know someone is a good manager? What is the definition of a good manager?*

When we ask these questions at our Effective Manager Conferences, we get all kinds of answers, such as the following:

- Their people like them.
- They communicate a lot.
- They're smart.
- They CARE.
- They listen well.
- They are respected.

These are good efforts, but they're still incorrect.

Suppose a manager reported to you who did or embodied all of the above, and for the past three years, *he had never achieved a single objective that the organization had set for him*. Would you describe him as a good manager? Of course you wouldn't.

Your First Responsibility as a Manager Is to Achieve Results

This may be the most important concept related to being a manager. Your first responsibility is NOT to your team of directs. It's NOT to your people. You should NOT worry about them first.

Your first responsibility is to deliver whatever results your organization expects from you. Whether you're a sales manager, and you have to "meet your numbers," or you're an accounting manager, and you have to "prepare the quarterlies," or you're a project manager, and you have to "deliver, on time, on budget, in scope," the thing that really matters is that you do what your company expects you to do.

For many managers, this creates a problem. You probably can't name your top five key results that you owe your organization this year. You most likely can't tick off on your fingers, *with ease*, the key things for which you're responsible. You may be able to say, "My boss wants me to focus in these areas," but that's not enough. You can't quantify what is expected of you.

About the only way to really feel good about what your responsibilities are is to have quantified goals, in numbers and percentages: "Higher than 92 percent call quality each week"; "Achieve 1.6 MM in sales"; "Maintain gross margins above 38 percent"; "Reduce shipping losses by 2.7 percent cumulatively year over year." (If not having these kinds of goals frustrates or worries you, perhaps you think that everyone else *has* clear goals. But don't worry. They probably don't either.)

The problem with not having clearly delineated responsibilities is that you can't make intelligent choices about where to focus. You begin to feel that "everything is important." You begin to "try to get everything done." Of course, you can't, and you probably know that already, because you're working long hours and never get everything done. You're not alone.

If you can't list your goals almost off the top of your head, make a note somewhere to go to your boss in the near future. Ask her: "What results do you expect of me?" "What are the measures you're going to compare me against?" "What are the objective standards?" "What subjective things do you look at to round out your evaluation of me?" (If you want to know more details about how to have this conversation, go to There's a Cast for That™.)

Take notes, and go back to your desk and figure out what actions you're going to take in order to deliver those results.

A lot of managers fear this conversation. The thinking goes, "If there are no measures, they can't use them against me." But that type of thinking is shortsighted. There are always measures. If you don't know what they are, they may be being used against you. Your boss is privately and subjectively evaluating you.

Okay, so results come first. Managers who produce great results have more successful careers than those who produce average results. But even reading this statement probably bothers you a little, because you've likely met at least one manager who gets great results and does well *whom you despise*. There are managers who put results so far ahead of everything else that they justify all sorts of behaviors to achieve those results. There are even industries— Wall Street comes to mind—that are more likely to tolerate this kind of behavior from managers. When the ends justify the means for managers, bad things happen to the workers who report to them.

A focus *only* on results far too often leads to abuse of workers. The worldwide labor movement—unions—traces its beginnings to soon after the beginning of . . . management. Managers were told, "Just get results," and they did so, at the expense of the health and safety of their employees. So, fairly soon, the workers joined forces.

Your Second Responsibility as a Manager Is to Retain Your People

Effectively managed modern organizations now measure *retention* in addition to results when they are evaluating a manager. It's intended to be a brake against an unrelenting results focus. They want to ensure that a manager's team members don't leave the organization.

Replacing employees is expensive. When someone leaves, there's the lost work that had been planned for, the cost of interviewing in both money and time, the likely higher salary that will be paid in the event of replacement, the time and expense of training the new employee, and the cost of less productivity by the new employee until that person can match the quality and quantity of work of the person who has left.

For today's manager, it's not enough to get results.

The Definition of an Effective Manager Is One Who Gets Results and Keeps Her People

In the best companies in the world, when executives get together to review the talent of their managers, the results and retention of managers are always at the heart of the discussion. When there's a discussion about who is best, who deserves a promotion, and who is "ready now" or going to be "ready next," these two metrics come up over and over again: *How well did this manager do her job, as shown in her results? Did she retain her people?*

If you want to be an effective manager and if you want to maximize your job security (and, I would argue, your professional satisfaction), you've got to achieve these two metrics. You've got to know how your organization (for results, it's usually your boss) measures them, and you've got to choose to spend your time on things that achieve them.

What are the things that you can DO that are most likely to achieve them?

2

The Four Critical Behaviors

[AUTHOR'S NOTE: IF YOU DON'T want to learn the fundamental principles that underlie my recommendations, and you think you're ready to dive right in to what to do and how to do it, you can skip this chapter and the next one, and go directly to Chapter 4, "Know Your People—One On Ones." I don't recommend it, but if you're impatient to get going, go.]

When my Manager Tools cofounder Mike Auzenne and I started our management careers, we had been taught very little about managing others. We struggled to learn what to do and how to do it, probably just the way you have struggled, and are doing so now. We didn't know that there are basically four things that great managers do a lot better than average and poor managers do. Once we understood these four things, we decided to start Manager Tools so that managers wouldn't have to learn the hard way, as we did.

The four critical behaviors that an effective manager engages in to produce results and retain team members are the following:

1. Get to Know Your People.
2. Communicate about Performance.

3. Ask for More.
4. Push Work Down.

Managers who get results and keep their people almost always do these four things much better than other managers do. (I say, "almost always" because there are exceptions. If you're incredibly smart—on the level of a Bill Gates, Andy Bechtolsheim, Warren Buffett, or Mike Morrisroe—you can probably get by just being smarter than everyone else. But, hey, you're probably not that smart. Mike and I sure aren't.)

The First Critical Behavior: Get to Know Your People

All of our data over the years show that the single most important (and efficient) thing that you can do as a manager to improve your performance and increase retention is to spend time getting to know the strengths and weaknesses of your direct reports. Managers who know how to get the most out of *each individual member of the team* achieve noticeably better results than managers who don't. The most efficient way to get to know your team is to spend time regularly communicating with them.

Despite the fact that your primary responsibility is getting results, the most important thing you can do *isn't* strategizing, task assignment, resource planning, or priority analysis. It's getting to know the people who have the skills and who are going to get the work done.

For the record, a manager *can* increase performance *in the short term* very effectively by using the power of his or her role as manager and threatening—and expecting—compliance. But if retention is thrown in as a required goal, that technique quickly sours.

Our data over the years suggest that, generally, a manager who knows his or her team members one standard deviation better than the average manager **produces results that are two standard deviations better** **than the average manager's results.**

Why is this, do you think? Think about your own relationship with your manager for a second. Do you want your boss to "treat you like everyone else"? Then, maybe you don't need to learn about your directs. However, I would guess that's not what you want. If you're a top performer, how would it feel to know that you were being managed just like your boss's weakest team member? If you were a weak performer, would you want the extra assign-ments that the top performer received on top of normal duties? Probably not.

Every person on the earth expects and deserves to be treated as an *individual.* Sadly, what most of us as managers do (I know I did early in my career) is *manage others the way we would like to be managed.* This is sort of the Golden Rule of nonexperienced managers. You do to your directs what would make sense if you were one of those directs.

The problem with this type of managing is that it only works (a little bit) with people a lot like you. Perhaps you're now a software development manager managing other developers. There's a pretty good chance that a good portion of your team is a lot like you. If you used to be a sales rep and are now a sales manager managing other sales reps, there's a lesser chance, but still a good one, that some members of your team are a lot like you. The problem with this is that it only works at the lowest levels and only for a little while. If you aspire to more, your Golden Rule is going to fail you.

People and their behaviors are what deliver results to your organization. (Not systems, not processes, not computers, not machines.) Results are your primary responsibility. We are all unique—every one of us. What makes any of us as managers think that one size could *ever* fit all? It might be easier, but it's not more effective. And, if you're worried that it takes a lot of work to be a good manager, this book will show you that it really doesn't.

If you're working for a boss who's different from you—he's outwardly passionate, and you're reserved and thoughtful, or she's smart and analytical, and you're a "people" person—your chances of success are diminished.

If you're going to manage people who are different from us—and you are, as team sizes continue to grow to save costs—we're going to have to learn to manage people who aren't like you. That means being willing to adjust depending on the person you're managing (just like you want your boss to do with you).

At this point, if you're like a good percentage of the hundreds of thousands of managers we've trained over the years, you're probably thinking one of two things:

1. I think I know my people very well, actually.
2. No need—I talk to my people all the time!

Let's take each of these ideas in turn. First, "I know my people very well." Perhaps you do, but the vast majority of managers who claim to really don't. I'd guess you think you do, but I would bet that you don't.

Here's a thought experiment to judge your own knowledge of your team members. First, what's more important to you: your family or your work? For most of you, the answer is family, and rightfully so.

Now, ask yourself the same question about your directs. What's more important to *them*: their family or their work? Without much thought, you realize that the answer is family first for them as well. And you'd be right—we've asked.

So, for your directs, their family is more important than work. You say that you know your directs very well. Here's a test of that knowledge.

What Are the First Names of All of the Children of the People Who Report Directly to You?

If you're like roughly 95 percent of the managers we ask this question, you *don't* know all of their names. A fair portion—maybe 40 percent—don't even know how many children all of their directs have! We call this, by the way, The Direct Relationship Acid Test. [There's a Cast for That™.]

This isn't a conclusive exercise, of course. But most people agree it's a reasonable indicator—a fair proxy. Think about it from the perspective of your personal life: your close friends all know the names of all of your children. That's part of what makes them close friends. Your friends who are not as close know some of your children. And your acquaintances probably don't know whether you have children or not.

If you failed the test, consider this: what makes you think you can get the last full measure of devotion to work out of someone when you don't know the names of the people who are the most precious to them in the world? In our experience, you probably can't. If you're smart and you work hard, you can do okay, but you're missing the biggest leverage of all: a trusting relationship with those whom you manage.

If you're responding to this discussion by thinking, "I'm not sure I like all the familiarity. I don't want to be friends with my directs," then you're not alone. A lot of managers do a lot of their work with their team by e-mail, or they see themselves as leaders rather than managers, or they say to themselves, "I didn't need to be 'managed,' and I don't want to have to manage my team; they should know what to do." We'll have more to say on this, but for now, our first recommendation is this: spending 30 minutes a week with each of your directs isn't likely to result in your becoming "friends" with them.

Now let's look at the second item mentioned earlier: "No need—I talk to my people all the time!" Many managers say this to us when we recommend that they spend focused, scheduled time getting to know their directs. They're constantly in communication with their directs through e-mail, texts, and plenty of face-to-face conversations. In fact, they feel like they talk to their directs so much that they hardly have time for their own work.

Most managers, however, have no idea how *one-sided* their conversations are with their team members. They have no idea how *little* influence those brief conversations actually have on building relationships.

Consider this: if you're like a lot of managers, you sit close to some or all of your team members. If this is true, it's very likely that you've been at your desk, in your office (or cubicle, or space) on a given day, and you've needed to communicate with a member of your team. You thought about sending an e-mail but then realized the team member was at her desk, so you thought you'd walk over and ask her about whatever it was you needed. You thought it would be good to chat, as well, and see how she was doing.

You walked over and asked, "Got a second?" and what did your direct almost definitely answer? "Sure!"

Well, your direct didn't answer that way because she thinks you're awesome. She answered that way because you're her boss. She knows you're probably not there just to chat. You're there because you want something. That's not a premise of a conversation that leads to a trusting relationship. It's very likely that whatever chit-chat you engage in with her—"How was your weekend?" "How's your spouse?" "What's the latest with the kids?"—is heard by them, to some extent, as *blah-blah-blah-I'm-going-to-get-to-the-real-reason-I'm-here-in-just-a-minute-blah-blah-blah*.

I'm not saying that you don't care about your direct's weekend, or their spouse, or their children. I know you do, but they have a different perception of your caring about them than you think they have if you generally only ask those questions before you're going to ask them for something.

Further, you don't realize the extent to which your chit-chat with them is driven by *you*, by your agenda, and by what you want. It's unlikely that many of your directs, when you stop by to see them, will automatically feel comfortable talking to you about anything at all.

Let me share a realization I've come to over the years after working with hundreds of thousands of managers. *Your directs don't see you as a nice person.* I'm not saying you're *not* a nice person—I believe you are, and your directs probably believe so, too. But that's not how your directs *see you. They see you as their boss.* It's a hard truth, but one worth remembering. Because of the power of your role, your directs don't see you the way you see yourself.

One way to think about this disparity in perception is to imagine that, for the vast majority of us managers, we have a sign on our forehead. It's visible to all of our directs, and it says, *Watch out. I'm your boss. I could fire you.* When you control others' addiction to food, clothing, and shelter, they're going to see you through a different lens than you see yourself.

If you doubt this, if you think that you're different—that you're loved and not feared at all by your team—think of it this way: *do you tell your boss everything?* Of course you don't.

And neither do your directs tell you everything—because you're their boss. Even if you're the nicest person you see in the mirror every morning, even if they would admit you're a really nice guy, to them, you're still the boss, and the power of your role distorts the relationship.

I used to show groups of managers whom our firm was training a videotape of managers interacting with their directs. It was only one minute long, comprising six 10-second video clips of two people meeting in a standard corporate hallway. The video clips were selected because they all showed a manager and a subordinate of the manager. It was a security camera video, with no sound, in black and white. The managers watching didn't know the people in the video clips, and the people in the video clips were dressed in standard corporate casual attire.

A quiz was given for each 10-second video clip to see, based only on demeanor, body language, and conversational interaction (again, *without sound*), which of the two people was the manager and which was the subordinate.

Every manager in every group got all of the answers right virtually every time. They could tell who was the manager, and you could have, too. Our role power as managers affects every interaction we have with our team members.

It's likely that, when you talk to your directs, you're blind to the effect that your role power has on them. Just because you're "chatting" doesn't mean you're building a relationship. What's happening in your directs' mind is probably closer to this: "I'm waiting for a task assignment."

To build a trusting relationship, it takes more than chit-chat, more than "talking to your people all the time." And the trust in this relationship matters a lot, according to our measures of effective managers. It takes even more trust building in a manager-subordinate relationship than it does with friends.

Generally, the more a team trusts its manager, the better the results will be, and the better the retention as well.

One of the best titles of a business book I've ever read is *The Speed of Trust*, written by Stephen M. R. Covey. If I trust my directs, I can spend less time telling them all the details about an assignment, checking their work, and asking for voluminous and frequent reports. Sure, I still have to check their work, and I still need to ask for the reports, but I spend a lot less time on both, and so do my directs. There's more time for accomplishing work that leads to results.

When I trust my boss, I spend less time worrying about what her intentions are and whether I have to cover my tail on all of my work. I don't have to second-guess the "why" of a task or the delegation of it, or ask my colleagues for political support if I decide to push back on something. There's more time for results.

Think about yourself and your "team" of directs. I put quotes on the word *team* because you and your directs really aren't, and can probably never be, a true team. That's not a popular thing to say these days, because everyone talks about teams all the time. But it's still true.

Think about this: what team were you ever on in which one of your teammates could kick you off the team? You might say, "Well, my school soccer coach could have kicked me off the team." *But your soccer coach wasn't part of the "team," was he?*

When we give managers an organizational chart showing the managers and their directs and we say, "Draw your team," the managers generally circle themselves and the team as a whole. But when we give that same instruction to the directs on that team, the directs circle themselves and their peers—and leave the manager out.

That's okay, because, for all of the talk of managers and their directs being a team, you don't actually need to be a true team. You need the ingredient that makes high-performance teams *high performing*.

Trust

The groundbreaking book by Jon R. Katzenbach and Douglas K. Smith, *The Wisdom of Teams,* taught us years ago that the binding and distinctive element of teams that outperform others is the amount of trust that they build and engender among their members. To get our group of directs performing more like a team, we've got to develop trusting relationships with them, despite the effect of our role power.

Psychologists tell us that building trust starts with communication. When you communicate with others, they evaluate your communications with them in two ways: quantity and quality. *Quantity* is the frequency of your communications. You communicate more with those whom you consider friends and trusted colleagues, and less with those with whom you have less of a relationship. The *quality* of our communications is judged by whether or not what we talk about is of interest or benefit *to them.*

If you're going to create trust and trusting relationships with your directs, then, you're going to have to *talk to them frequently about things that are important to them.*

Can you see both the quality and the quantity portion of that guidance? You've got to "talk to them frequently": that's the quantity portion. And you've got to talk to them "about things that are important to them": that's the quality portion. Hopefully, you can see that saying "I talk to my people all the time!" isn't enough, because you're talking about things that are important to *you.*

[**Author's Note:** For the record, there's an important implicit assumption in all of our Manager Tools' work: *you are an ethical, trustworthy person.* I've tried repeatedly to write guidance about how my recommendations would change to address the selfish people in power who are willing to cheat a bit here and there, lie a little in reports, treat others as tools, and, by doing so, get ahead (for themselves). I can't figure out how to do it, and so I won't. If you're one of those people, you can stop reading now, because you won't like my recommendations.]

Before we move on to a discussion of the second critical behavior, "communicating about performance," it's important to note that the four critical behaviors are not weighted equally. The four behaviors don't each account for 25 percent of the total value of the Four Effective Behaviors.

Getting to know your directs accounts for 40 percent of the total value created by engaging in the four critical behaviors.

That's right: your relationship with your directs, based on all the work we have done and all the data we have collected, is by far the most important thing you can do to improve results and retention.

As an engineer by schooling from the Military Academy, I was someone who didn't really "get" the importance of relationships and people when I first started my management career. Frankly, I didn't want to believe the early data we got from managerial behavior changes. I wanted management to be more about performance communications (which we'll talk about shortly).

But every time we've tested managers on "communicating about performance" without them having "developed relationships," we got poor results. The data said the same thing every time: the most important thing you can do as a manager is to develop a trusting relationship with the people on your team. If you do, everything else is easier. If you don't, everything else is harder, and your results will be attenuated.

The Second Critical Behavior: Communicate about Performance

Would your performance improve if you heard more often from your boss about how you were doing? Most professionals, when we ask them that question, give a resounding yes.

We also ask the following question: "Provided it was done politely and professionally, would you like more feedback and input from your boss and/or organization about your performance, on a more regular basis, regardless of whether it was positive or negative?"

Again, the answer is a resounding *yes*. Many folks actually go further and say, "She doesn't even need to tell me I'm doing well! If she would just professionally talk to me when I make mistakes rather than staying silent, I'd love that!" (Our data show that only giving negative input actually doesn't work very well over time. Directs begin to resent their boss for focusing on the negatives, even if they've asked for it.)

If you want more performance communications from YOUR boss, you know your directs want the same thing from you. [As a general rule, whatever you're thinking you'd like from your boss, it's likely that your directs want the same thing from you. Far too many bosses have this unsustainable thought: "Well, my boss doesn't do what *I* want *her* to do, but *my* people—they LOVE me." I'm sorry, but, while that's possible, it's really unlikely in Manager Tools' experience.]

Now, if you're like most managers, you don't talk to your team members very much about their performance. You're of the general mind-set that "They know how they're doing" or "If I have a real problem with them, I'll tell them" or "I don't need to praise them when they do something right! That's just them doing their job!" (We'll talk about praise and punishment later.)

When you think about it, everything that's done at a high level is done with a lot of communication about performance. If you've ever paid attention to the advertisements for high-performance cars, you've noticed that they all say (and it's true), "You can feel the road as you drive." That feeling is important in high-performance driving: knowing what the car is doing, what the road feels like. You have to adjust. The input about the road from the car that allows you to adjust is the feedback the car transmits to your hands on the wheel (and, according to drivers, your butt in the driver's seat).

Think about professional sports: football, American football, baseball. All things being equal, if you're like most fans, you'd prefer to watch professional games rather than high school games (unless your child is playing). The reason is that the caliber of play is much higher. You want to see something done well—done expertly. At times, play at the highest level approaches beauty.

One of the underlying reasons for that beauty is the athletes who perform at the highest levels of the game are provided with feedback about their performance for their entire career. Major League Baseball shortstops and second basemen—the very best in the world at their jobs—still go to spring training every year and practice, practice, practice. They regain their timing and teamwork through repetition: *they take action and pay attention to the feedback they get.* One baseball player once said that he thought they turned 5,000 double plays every spring—5,000!—when, in a normal season, turning 150 would be an outstanding accomplishment! Why that amount of practice? They know that creating and using the feedback that they receive will make them better, when it matters.

Even the technology we use every day relies on communication about its performance. Every machine we interact with—smartphones, tablets, cars, computers, televisions—all have numerous feedback circuits built into them. They're constantly checking themselves for being within tolerance, checking variances, within normal limits, to avoid a significant failure.

About the only part of human endeavor in which feedback isn't rapid, frequent, and timely is management. Just about the only place where feedback isn't given, isn't used, isn't taken for granted is between managers and their directs. We all say that, as directs, we want feedback, but it usually just isn't forthcoming.

When we talk to high-performing directs who rate their boss as outstanding, performance communications come up over and over again as a core reason. "He tells me how I'm doing." "When I do well, he says so." "When I mess up, he quickly tells me, and we move on." "I never need to worry about where I stand—she tells me."

I'll never forget one manager telling me, "I didn't know that communicating about performance was super important for getting great results. I just did it because it was what I would have wanted. I didn't like it in the beginning, but it worked, and I got over that."

If you want high performance, you're going to have to talk about it with your directs. It matters more than anything else, other than your relationship with them.

Performance communication accounts for 30 percent of the total value created by engaging in the four critical behaviors.

This means that, if you build a great relationship with each of your directs and talk with them about performance regularly, you're 70 percent of the way to getting results and retaining your team.

The Third Critical Behavior: Ask for More

Our data show that, if you want great results and retention, you have to be willing to constantly raise the bar on performance. It's not enough, based on what we see, to simply be a caretaker. It's not enough to accept from your directs what their "comfort zone" is. It's not enough to let your directs "stay where they are."

I can assure you, executives at your firm don't think anybody should be in their "comfort zone" very often. Executives are in a constant state of stress and expect something similar (and sustainable) from you and your team. Executives are completely justified in thinking this way. If your company or industry is growing or changing (and "changing" includes "shrinking"), then every job is changing as well. It's the manager's job to figure out what the external change means for her group and to direct the performance of her group in ways that satisfy the needs of the organization.

You've probably heard the phrase, "I'm stressed out." You've probably even said it yourself. Well, this may surprise you: as managers, we're *supposed* to stress out our directs. Yes, you read that correctly. You're supposed to create stress for your directs.

How is this possible? Well, what most people don't know about stress is that there are two kinds. There's *distress*: that's the kind you mean when you're feeling "stressed out." It's a level of stress that impedes or hinders your performance. You're overwhelmed, you can't think straight, and you feel fearful, uncreative—frozen, even.

Think of stress, however, as occurring on a continuum (it does). Below the "stressed out" level of distress is the useful level of stress called *eustress*. It's pronounced "you-stress," and that *eu-* prefix is like the prefixes on euphoria, euphony, and eudaimonia. Eustress is the stress you feel that helps you get ready, get excited, and "get up" for the big game. It's that tingly feeling of anticipation, eagerness, and a sense of fire and determination that you feel when your team huddles and shouts, "Team!" or, "Beat Navy!" before a game.

The ideal place for your directs to be for maximum output/results is right on the line between distress and eustress, *almost* over the line into fear, but not quite there. They should have lots of energy but not panic. *The only way to know where that line is, for each direct, is to push each direct into moments of distress and pay attention to when they start to lose effectiveness.* Everyone has his or her own point of diminishing returns.

The way you do that is to ask for more.

If you're an experienced manager, you've probably dealt with a direct who says, "I'm happy where I am." Lots of new managers have been stumped by the average performer who doesn't want to improve and doesn't want a promotion, yet is still "technically doing the job." Not well, mind you, but the direct is meeting the standards.

As managers, we're responsible not just for the status quo, but for *improving* the performance of the whole team. The best way a team's performance improves is if each individual's performance improves. If your team's goals are being raised (and, if they aren't right now, I assure you that someone is thinking about raising them), you need to get more out of everyone to meet those higher goals.

So, the direct who says he is happy where he is fine, for now. In a year, though, his job will have changed enough—and the standards will have risen enough, because standards are always rising—that *his performance will have declined relative to the needs of the job.* [There's a Cast for That™: My Direct Doesn't Want to Change.]

The effective manager is always, in one fashion or another, asking for more. To be an effective manager means encouraging and inspiring all of your directs to higher performance even when they say they don't want to—because you know the organization needs that to stay competitive.

Asking for more accounts for roughly 15 percent of the total value created by engaging in the four critical behaviors.

The Fourth Critical Behavior: Push Work Down

Manager Tools gets asked frequently, "Why are there four parts to your 'Management Trinity'?" Well, it's not like a couple of engineers can't do math. And it's certainly not marketing. (We're horrible at marketing.)

The reason "pushing work down" is the fourth part of our "Management Trinity" is that, while the first three parts of the "Management Trinity" create value for the team, "pushing work down" creates *capacity for the organization.* Managers are the ones who have to push work down, but the organization is the one that benefits. Put differently, you can produce results from your team with only the first three parts of the "Management Trinity," but pushing work down creates growth potential for your entire organization.

What does it mean to "push work down"? Here's a simple way to think about it. Suppose there's a task that both you and one of your directs can do. You usually do it, but your directs—or at least one of them—COULD do the task. Maybe not as well as you, but close enough that the quality of the work would be acceptable.

If I were leading a class in Managerial Economics 101, based on the above situation, I would give a quiz: "If the above situation is true, which of the two of you—your direct or you—SHOULD accomplish the task, and why?"

If you don't know the answer immediately, it's okay. But there is, in Managerial Economics 101, a right answer. *The direct should do the job and not the manager, because the direct is cheaper labor. If we can achieve an acceptable quality level with less cost, for all but the most important things we do, we should do so.*

Why is this true? Because yes, directs are less expensive labor. That's not a rude statement—no insult is implied or should be inferred. Think of it this way: if you had a choice of hiring two contractors, or workers of any type, and you knew they would provide work of roughly equal quality, wouldn't you hire the less expensive one? Of course you would.

Now, a lot of directs would say, "Well, yes, technically I'm cheaper, but that's not the whole story. I have my own work to do! I don't have time for my manager to push work down to me. I'm already fully busy."

They're right, but that's not a defense against work being pushed down. Why? Because the question really isn't whether people are busy or not. *All workers are* busy, aren't they? By using the defense of "busyness," no work would ever be transferred to anyone else, and we would all be stuck in a weird productivity stasis (which, due to the link between productivity and profitability, and the inevitability of change, is the equivalent of an organizational death spiral).

The question becomes, in a world in which everyone is busy with too much to do, "What work is most valuable to the organization?" That's the work we have to get done, right? And, in a general sense, the more important work of the organization is being done at higher levels. (If you're a software developer, or a former software developer, that probably irritates you, but the data don't support your contention that what you do is the most important thing the company does.)

What this means for us managers is that we have to learn to share our work (that which we can share, which is probably most of it) with our directs.

There's an even more important (though admittedly organizational) reason why we need to learn to push work down, but we'll discuss that in a later chapter.

Pushing work down accounts for roughly 15 percent of the total value created by engaging in the four critical behaviors.

■ ■ ■

That's the "Management Trinity": The four most critical behaviors a manager can engage in, to produce results and retain team members:

1. Get to Know Your People.
2. Communicate about Performance.
3. Ask for More.
4. Push Work Down.

Teachable and Sustainable Tools

YOU'VE PROBABLY NOTICED THAT I haven't talked yet about the core Manager Tools: One On Ones (O3s), Feedback, Coaching, and Delegation. That's because *you don't need to use our tools to become a great manager*.

You don't need to use our One-On-One, Feedback, Coaching, or Delegation Tools in order to achieve great results and retain your team. Our tools, delineated in this book, as well as our podcasts and our work with clients all over the world, *aren't the only way* to achieve the four critical behaviors: Know Your People, Talk about Performance, Ask for More, and Push Work Down.

Put differently, you may be able to achieve the four key behaviors in your own way, with techniques you've developed on your own over the course of your career. You don't "have" to use our One-On-One Tool to get to know your people. You don't "have" to use our Feedback Tool to talk about performance, and so forth.

If you've got your own way, and you're achieving the four critical behaviors, leading to great results and team member retention, you're good to go. *Almost*. Unfortunately, it's not quite enough to use the four critical behaviors and achieve your two fundamental responsibilities.

However you manage, your techniques, behavior, and philosophy *must be both teachable to others and sustainable.*

What does this mean? It means that you have to be able to teach others how to do what you do, and you have to be able to continue to apply those same teachable behaviors and externally visible skills and abilities, in different roles, in different organizations, through different economic conditions, wherever you are, for long periods of time.

Consider the following scenario, the underpinnings of which are fairly common in organizations everywhere. Suppose you are a process engineering manager in a manufacturing facility. You have four process engineers reporting to you. Your team does analysis of production and fabrication processes throughout the plant, coming up with better, faster, and cheaper ways to produce a high-quality final product.

One of your directs is very good at his job. He can solve most problems, at least as well as anyone else on your team, and often better. Unfortunately, he considers himself "a very private person," especially about his work. When you ask him to come up with a solution to a problem, he usually goes into his office, closes the door, and works by himself for a day or two, depending on the problem. He won't ask for input, won't collaborate, and won't share drafts of his work. He will just come up with a solution.

If you have questions about how he got to his solution, he says, "I can't really describe it. I just think about it for a while, and the solution comes to me." When you ask him to share his concepts at a staff meeting, he shrugs his shoulders and says, "It's just the way I do things. It won't make much sense to anyone else." When you ask him to train a new team member, he tells the team member, "I don't think I can tell you much about what I do. It's kind of my personality."

I submit that you wouldn't tolerate this for very long. It's really not enough for someone merely to get the job done. The team member has to be able to talk about it, communicate about it, and explain it, and even defend it if need be. If something goes wrong, you may have to ask that team member to walk through their process step-by-step as part of a root cause analysis.

Interesting

We don't really think about it very often, but the way in which people do their work matters, at some level. We expect people in finance, say, to be able to explain the functions they put into a spreadsheet and why. We expect engineers to be able to walk us through why they chose a particular design or a material. We expect developers to comment their code so that someone else can debug it. We expect marketing people to explain their rationale for why they chose a certain data-gathering campaign.

But somehow we don't hold managers to this standard. Somehow, with all the work being done about people, systems, motivation, pay, benefits, rewards, and culture, "management" is some sort of inexplicable "black art." Managers aren't expected to be able to explain how they manage. When I ask managers to explain how they manage, many just shrug their shoulders and say, "I don't know." The good ones do so and grin about it. The bad ones go on to say, "It's not like anybody ever taught me. The company doesn't really help us out, you know."

Sometimes in my work with clients, I hear them say, "Nobody ever taught me. I just learned what to do from previous bosses." When I say, "Oh, you had good bosses who set the right example—that's good," their reply is something along the lines of, "I didn't say *that* . . . "

What does it say about the most important systemic behavior in every organization that the majority of us learned how to do it from others *who were never taught it and who privately worried that others would discover that they didn't truly know what they were doing?*

A large portion of the answers we get at Manager Tools to the question, "What's your approach to managing?" is "It's just who I am." Or, "It's my personality."

Think about what that "personality" answer means in this situation. You're a relatively reserved technical person who is very good at her job. In fact, you're probably the best QA (quality assurance) person on your team. You're methodical, logical, careful, and take great pride in the quality of your work. You're not really very social at work, but you have close friends with whom you spend time at home, and you are known to them as a good friend and a good listener.

Your boss, on the other hand, is the complete opposite of you. He's "sales-y." He's outgoing, cheerful, chatty, knows everyone, and is comfortable in front of a crowd. He knows everyone's favorite Starbucks order. And, he's a good manager. A little messy at times, sure. He sometimes starts something and doesn't finish it, but he spends time with everyone on the team. He knows each person's strengths and weaknesses. He's smart. He stays positive, and he is a very good motivator, too.

A while back, your boss told you how well you were doing. He said he was impressed with your professionalism and liked how you were a team player. He mentioned that his boss thought you might be management material.

You told him that you *had* been thinking about the next steps in your career but that you had questions. You asked him, "What makes you a good manager?" His answer was, "Glad you asked! Basically, I'm pretty sure it's just my personality. I'm outgoing. I like people. I like talking with people. I keep my eye on the big picture. I don't know; it's kind of a gift, I guess."

With this answer from your boss, *you were pretty certain that you'd never be able to be a manager, because you and your boss were polar opposites.* You didn't have his "gift," and you certainly weren't "outgoing." You weren't thought of as being great with people, except maybe by your friends. Your boss made it seem as if managing is about traits and characteristics, not about behavior, skills, or abilities. You believed that you needed to be the type of person who caused other people to say about you, "She's a people person."

I can assure you, if the CEO or VP of Human Resources at your firm had known that that conversation had taken place, that CEO or VP would have been angry with your boss. He might have said: "*We need every effective person to think about growing their skills and influencing more people in the firm. We can't create a ghetto of non-managers just because they're not 'like you.' Maybe not everybody wants to be a manager, but if someone wants to or is willing to consider it, we ought not to discourage that person. There are all kinds of great managers who are reserved or even shy. Managing is about results and retention, not about smiling and knowing people. Sure, it's a people job, but it's a job that any person can do with the right skills and behaviors! Don't stunt your people's possibilities because they're not you! Our chief information officer (CIO) is as different from our chief marketing officer (CMO) as any two people ever can be in terms of personality, but, wow, do they both get things done! One's an introvert, and the other is so outgoing, it's annoying. And their staffs love working for them both. We can't build on your 'personality.' That's not sustainable.*"

The way an effective manager manages is visible to others and is teachable to others. And the effective manager can repeat the core behaviors in any situation, nearly anywhere.

The reasons for this are fundamental to any organization. If we can't teach others how to manage, it's much harder for the organization to grow. We can't teach "personality," and we can't teach "I don't know."

When your organization's business or service grows, at some point more managers are going to be needed. If the people who are considered for promotion to a newly created managerial role haven't learned how to manage *well* from their own manager, they're not going to be any good at it. And just when the organization needs additional effectiveness in order to sustain its growth, that effectiveness not there.

To sustain organizational growth, new managers must be created, and the way to create new managers is to teach them *before* they move into the role. Otherwise, they will learn the hard way—when they're already in the role. And that means learning from their own mistakes, at a time when the organization doesn't need *new, weak managers* but, rather, managers as good as the ones they already have—and *better*—before the growth. The newer managers have to be better because, as organizations grow, growth becomes more difficult, so the same behaviors in a more difficult situation begets less performance just when more is needed.

Knowing that there is a need for teachable and sustainable skills caused me to start creating the foundations for Manager Tools' guidance. I'd been hearing for years that managers didn't feel good about their performance. They wanted to get better but didn't know how.

Managers would read books, but most were too vague. The books had good ideas, but the managers didn't know *what to do* when they finished reading the books. I remember reading *In Search of Excellence* before I left the Army and being both thrilled at the insights and disappointed that *the book didn't tell me what to do or how to do it.* Of course, the book wasn't really meant for frontline managers. But I couldn't find any books that were. So I read the book that everyone else was reading. As you've probably experienced, this is still true of most management books.

I was seeing that too many managers couldn't sustain a short-term success, or, if the business environment changed, they couldn't adapt. Of those who were thought to be good managers, too many of them couldn't explain what they did or how they did it.

Because I knew about the four critical *behaviors* (not personality, not schooling, not traits, not attributes), I started refining the methods and tools that I believed would help managers achieve them. I developed models, tested them, and paid attention to results from client executives and managers. Over the course of about seven years, I developed the four tools for the four critical behaviors that we call the "Management Trinity." We have been teaching them for twenty years.

Here's an example of how Manager Tools One On Ones (MTO3s) took shape by working with client executives and managers. A general manager of a large manufacturing organization called me with a request for help. His line of business was beginning to show signs of a struggle. He said that this division of a Fortune 500 firm had grown quickly, and he was having to work too hard on getting his vision out and struggling to find out how things were going. He was being surprised by operational misses and delays. He was about to squeak by on his goals for the quarter, after three to four quarters of being certain about being able to beat his forecasts. He felt that his managers—426 in total, throughout several levels— were overwhelmed by the technical and logistical systems that the organization had to put in place in order to handle the volume increases with which they were dealing.

When I interviewed 30 to 40 managers to find out what was going on, I kept getting bad answers to questions about communications. Lower-level workers weren't hearing about changes until they were forced to deal with them. Managers were not told about potential market changes that would lead to product changes that would lead to operational changes in their area. There was little knowledge of some of the cost-cutting efforts that were starting.

My client and I had both read *High Output Management* by Andy Grove and thought One On Ones might be a great tool to create more communication. We tweaked Andy's idea and started having managers at all levels do weekly 30-minute One-On-One meetings. We thought that managers should get to know their directs and give

purpose of O3s

them a regularly scheduled forum for their questions and concerns, which would allow the manager to share what was going on and perhaps give some guidance and feedback.

To make things simple, we decided to split the 30 minutes into two 15-minute segments. We also set it up so that the manager would speak first. Managers always speak first in meetings, right?

It was a disaster. Within three months, we stopped the effort. We had been tracking results and various other factors, and in that little time—roughly 90 days—we were already seeing declines in areas in which we didn't want to see them. Managers actually liked the meetings somewhat, *but the directs absolutely hated them.*

When we asked the directs why they didn't like the meetings, most of the answers we received were variations on a theme: "Just another meeting with my boss." "This isn't a meeting for 'us.'" "Just more work being assigned to me."

We also learned something else that astounded us. Remember one of the two primary reasons that managers push back on spending focused time with their directs in One On Ones is "I talk to my people all the time!"? Well, apparently that wasn't exactly true. The average length of time that managers talked in this not-necessary meeting with their directs-with-whom-they-were-always-talking was *28 minutes out of the scheduled 30.* They said they didn't need any more time with their directs, and then they proceeded to talk their ears off.

Why did the directs hate the meetings? Because they had been told that it was going to be a joint meeting and that it was an opportunity for them to develop a stronger, trusting relationship with their boss. This clearly didn't happen. In fact, what do you think most directs said when the manager looked at the time and said, "Oh, I've taken 28 minutes. Do you have anything for me?" Of course, the directs said, "No," which meant this meeting wasn't about "me" or "us" at all.

We found, however, some other data buried in our results. One senior director, who had 24 managers in his organization, had gotten great results. Where the larger group had seen declines, this manager and his subordinate managers had improved performance metrics and were loving their One On Ones.

When we interviewed the senior director and some of his managers, we discovered that he had changed the organizational guidelines slightly. He had basically said, "I'm kind of lazy, and I don't want to prep for another meeting, *so I'll just let the directs go first rather than me*." All of his managers followed suit.

The directs loved it. They rated their relationship with their manager better within three months, whereas the directs in the other group's meetings, in which the managers went first, described a decline in their relationship with their manager. Managers loved it, too, because they still got to cover whatever they wanted to cover, every week.

Here's what might surprise you: the directs, going first in the 30-minute meeting, *talked on average 28 minutes*: the same amount of time as the managers talked when they went first in the other group's meetings.

There's no way a group can logically sustain saying "We already talk enough" if, when you give them a chance to talk in an already busy schedule, they fill up the agenda and then some.

So, when we talk about One On Ones, you'll note that the direct goes first.

We then expanded our work with One On Ones at an even bigger corporate client. The organization was a large division, with 1,100 managers. We tested a rough equivalent of our current guidelines.

We had 700 managers in the test group practice One On Ones (some weekly, some biweekly, some monthly). We had 400 managers in a control group, who continued to manage the way they always had. They were forbidden from doing O3s.

The study was scheduled to run for 30 months. Unfortunately, and frustratingly, we had to stop the test after only 19 months. The reason was that because 18 months into our test, unrelated to the test, a corporate document was distributed, showing which managers had been promoted to which roles in the past 12 months. *Of the 43 managers promoted, 42 of them came from the test group, and only one came from the control group.*

Although you might think this was a validation of our effort and justification for continuing or even expanding the effort, a month later we had to shut down the study. Why? Because the managers in the control group, who also wanted to get promoted, started doing O3s as well, which ruined the science involved in our study.

However, 18 months was long enough to capture some of the outcomes we had hoped to track. Results and retention among managers in the test group rose by 9 percent and 8 percent, respectively. Results and retention among the control group rose slightly, by 1 percent.

The results get even better. Remember that in the test group there were different periodicities (weekly, biweekly, and monthly)? We also broke out those data.

Here's the rank ordering of results and retention improvements by periodicity:

1. Weekly—Biggest improvement in both results and retention
2. Biweekly—Slightly less than half the improvement seen by weekly O3s
3. No One On Ones—Slight improvement in results and retention
4. Monthly—*Slight decrease in results and retention*

If the monthly results and retention scores were included in the test group's averages (they were, because we thought they would also

TABLE 3.1   Four Specific Manager Tools to Address the Four Critical Behaviors

Critical Behavior	Manager Tool
Get to Know Your People	One On Ones
Communicate about Performance	Feedback
Ask for More	Coaching
Push Work Down	Delegation

increase), the monthly One On Ones actually held back the overall average improvement of the test group.

If we hadn't tested monthly One On Ones (and, believe me, we don't recommend them), the results and retention improvement shown by the test group would have been even higher.

I'll explain why we think that is the case when we talk about One On Ones in the next chapter.

After many years of testing all of the tools the way we did the One On Ones, we crafted four specific tools to address the four critical behaviors, as shown in Table 3.1.

As I've said before, these tools aren't the only way to be an effective manager. You may have your own tools, your own way. If you're getting results and retaining your team, and your methods are teachable and sustainable, well done! I suspect you know by now that you're pretty rare as a manager.

However,

- If you don't really feel like you know what you're doing
- If you don't have your own technique
- If your technique is your personality
- If you can't teach others your technique

- If you can't write down your methods
- If you're not certain you could replicate your technique and methods in a different company/industry

Then here is Manager Tools' guarantee to you:

Use the Manager Tools as described here, and we guarantee that you will become an effective manager—one who gets results and retains the team.

4

Know Your People—One On Ones

MANAGER TOOLS RECOMMENDS THAT YOU hold One On Ones with each of your directs. What is a Manager Tools One On One? It is a meeting

That is *scheduled*

That is held *weekly*

That *lasts for 30 minutes*

That is *held with each of your directs*

In which *the direct's issues are primary*

In which *the manager takes notes*

Let's take each one of these components in turn and discuss why we recommend them.

Scheduled

Scheduling One On Ones means setting up a recurring appointment with each of your directs so that each of them is set to have the O3 with you at the same time every week.

Scheduling your O3s is actually more important than having them weekly. That's why it's first on our list. It is more important to schedule your One On Ones than to have One On Ones almost every week that are unscheduled. The value of having One On Ones is that by doing this you are saying to your directs, "You're always going to have time with me. I'm always going to be investing in the relationship." If you don't schedule your One On Ones, you're saying to your directs, "This might be important in a given week. You might be important, and the time with me might be valuable to me. I don't know. Let's play it by ear. We'll see how things go."

We originally thought that frequency of O3s would be more important than the scheduling of them, but we were wrong.

Here's what our research showed. (We've repeated similar results three times.) If we compare two groups of 100 managers who actually conduct O3s, *the managers who schedule their O3s outperform (against results and retention) the unscheduled managers by significant margins (as much as three to four times)*. What's more, it's really difficult to conduct O3s if you don't schedule them.

Take a look at the Table 4.1. We wanted to find out whether scheduling One On Ones was important. In order to do that, we wanted to compare two similarly sized groups of managers: those that did schedule their O3s, and those that didn't.

The first thing we learned was that it was much harder to actually *do* O3s if you didn't *schedule* O3s. We only had to assess 119 managers who scheduled their O3s to find 100 who then *did*

TABLE 4.1   Scheduled O3s vs. Unscheduled O3s

	Scheduled	Unscheduled
Managers Surveyed	119	520
Managers Tested	≈100	≈100
Improvement	≈8 percent	≈2 percent

them. But we had to survey over 500 managers who *said* they did O3s to find 100 that had actually conducted them significantly enough to be useful. (Our data show that if you conduct O3s 85 percent of the time, you get the kinds of results and retention you expect. Fall below 85 percent, and outcomes decline.)

This ought to ring true with most present-day managers' busy schedules. If it's not on your calendar, it's unlikely to get done. If you don't schedule One On Ones, they're just not going to happen. (And we have plenty of anecdotes of directs telling us, "I wish he hadn't even said he was going to do them. He never did, and it was worse than not trying at all.")

Here's what astounded us about the results of this survey. Even if you *did have* your O3s but did not schedule them, you would get nowhere near the improvement you would get if you scheduled them and stuck to your schedule.

Why is scheduling so important? Directs whose managers have started O3s tell us two key things: (1) "My boss is saying I'm important," and (2) "I have time to prepare."

1. "My Boss is Saying I'm Important."

Your directs struggle to get time with you, much like you struggle to get time with your own boss. The reason you give your directs for them not being able to get your time is often because you're in meetings all day, which, while regrettable, is true. They get that your calendar matters, but to them it's an impediment to getting their questions answered, their problems solved, and their ideas heard.

When you tell your directs that they're going to have scheduled time with you every week, no matter what, *you elevate their importance to that of the rest of the items on your calendar; that is, you are making them also "important."*

You might be thinking, "But I really do think my people are important!" I know you do. And, there's a difference in how important you think they are, and how important *they think* you think they are. At some point, for most directs, in fact, a boss who (a) doesn't have time for them and (b) says "you're important" is a bit like all the firms who say, "Our people are our most important asset." In many big firms, those kinds of tag lines become cynical jokes.

2. "I Have Time to Prepare."

You may have always told yourself that your directs get time to talk to you every day, when you stop by their desks to chat. But that's not how they see it, based on our interviews with directs all over the world. When you stop by their desks to chat, you do some chit-chat, and then you discuss whatever you stopped by for. Directs know this, and they don't assume that your stopping by randomly means it is an open forum to bring up ideas, issues, or concerns.

Directs also are uncomfortable about bringing up something formal or something that requires planning while you are hanging around their desk. Some topics require thinking through the issues and asking questions in a certain way. Most directs don't think, "My boss is going to stop by my desk today; I need to pitch him the idea I've been thinking about."

Directs tell us that having scheduled time with them on your calendar allows them to prepare for the meeting.

A lot of managers resist our guidance on scheduling their O3s. The first pushback we get is, "Well, that's great, but I can't keep to a schedule—my schedule is always changing." But here's what our research has shown: *moving an already scheduled One On One to a different time because of a conflict has no statistically significant effect on the manager's results and retention improvements.* Managers who schedule and then move their O3s frequently achieve similar improvements in results and retention as managers whose schedules are more fixed and rarely move their O3s.

Perhaps more importantly, *directs tell us that they don't care if you move the meeting.* They understand about schedules—that they often need to be rescheduled. But they also say that, if you use the excuse, "My schedule is too fluid," in order not to schedule O3s, to them this means the same (whether you mean it or not) as "I'm not going to have O3s."

You may also be thinking, "I'm too busy." This is a rational response to another meeting in your already busy day, but part of the reason your schedule is so full is because you're not spending enough time communicating with your directs. You're using e-mail too much, so you're having a lot of miscommunications.

I know you're busy, and squeezing five hours of meetings (assuming you have 10 directs) into your schedule this week or next is nearly impossible. You'd probably be right if you said, "It can't be done."

Fair enough. But let's try an experiment. Look at your calendar, but not for this week, or next week, or even the week after that. Look at your calendar three to four weeks from now. It's mostly empty, isn't it? Your calendar is "always full" because you're generally only looking at the current week. [There's a Cast for That™. Lots of them actually.] That's how calendars work: they fill up one to two weeks in advance. You're "always busy" because your daily (and probably current weekly) calendar is always full.

This means that you're probably not controlling your calendar effectively and entering meetings that are a priority on your calendar first. Our data show that time with your directs is the most important time that you will spend at work.

You don't have time now—that's understood—but the solution is easy. *Don't start your O3s for three to four weeks, when you can easily fit them into a calendar that is almost empty.* We'll talk about how and when to schedule One On Ones when we talk about announcing and rolling them out in Chapter 5.

And, finally, if you talk to managers who use Manager Tools One On Ones, they'll tell you that they *will never go back to not having them because they're too valuable.*

This leads us to the Manager Tools One-On-One Guarantee:

If you implement Manager Tools One On Ones, we guarantee that you will get more time back in your calendar than you spend in having them.

Yes, you're reading that right. The amount of time you spend in Manager Tools One On Ones—that you don't think you have time for right now!—will actually cause you to have more time to get more of your work done. How is that possible? You'll develop more trust with your directs. They'll know more often what you expect, because they'll be hearing it more regularly, so they won't ask you as many questions. You won't get interrupted as often for non-urgent issues. Your directs will wait to bring things to you that can wait. Have you ever noticed that a lot of the interruptions you get don't seem worthy of the time it takes to resolve them? That will diminish significantly once you start MTO3s.

We guarantee it.

Weekly

It is best to conduct your One On Ones on a weekly basis. The simplest reason for this is that you probably think about your work life in weekly increments. (According to research, it's roughly a three- to five-day window). You think about deadlines that are coming up *this week.* You tend to put off things that are due next week, even if they will take you several hours of work. You probably know what your schedule is this week, and maybe you know a bit of what your schedule is next week, but for the week after next, you have little sense of what your week will be like, in most cases.

Your directs tend to work the same way, for the most part. They think about their week when they're thinking about work. Things that are happening next week aren't very important. Two weeks from now seems like "the future."

Biweekly

What would it say to your directs if you scheduled biweekly One On Ones? Would it say to them that your directs are less important to you than what you're working on now? We've asked; that's what they told us. Here is a common response: "Meeting with my boss every other week, when everything else is done weekly, feels like he's putting me on the 'back burner'."

I'm not going to fall on my sword because I'm against biweekly O3s. (I'll save that for monthly O3s.) If your results are like our data, you'll get some improvement in results and retention: roughly 25 percent of what you would get if you held them weekly. Why would you save only 50 percent of time by going biweekly and then lose 75 percent of its value? That doesn't make sense.

You could decide to hold the One On Ones for one hour every other week, thereby spending the same amount of time in total. But that doesn't work nearly as well, generally speaking. Our data show that managers who do this end up with a compliance rate that is even less than that of managers who decide to have hourly O3s every week, and that compliance rate isn't great. Our conclusion is that managers who decide that they don't have time to have weekly O3s because they're "too busy" are going to use the same rationale for canceling close to 50 percent of their biweekly O3s.

Directs tell us over and over again that they prefer having weekly O3s. It matches the rhythm of their work. They say that biweekly O3s end up being too general and less relevant.

There's another benefit to holding weekly O3s that is lost if you go to biweekly O3s: *a significant reduction in interruptions*. If you're not doing One On Ones now, and you're like a lot of managers, you probably get interrupted frequently by your directs. They "have a quick question," or they "just need a minute." And that minute often turns out to be 10 minutes.

Those interruptions will be notably decreased when you start meeting on a regularly scheduled basis with your directs. (This is part of the reason for our guarantee regarding how much time you'll get back in your calendar.) Directs whom we've surveyed in every test commented on how they started waiting until their O3s to bring up issues, questions, or problems. If they had a problem Tuesday, and their O3 was scheduled for Thursday morning, they would probably wait to bring it up then. (The reason many interruptions seem urgent to your directs is that they have waited as long as they could.)

If you have your One On Ones biweekly, you will lose the benefit of seeing interruptions notably decrease. Directs can't wait over a week to meet with you in order to have their problems resolved. In my personal experience, in all of my One On Ones, at least half of them (and perhaps as many as three quarters) start with one of my directs saying, "My list is [long or short] this week." That tells me they're keeping a running list. If I weren't having my O3s, each item on the list would be an interruption, or another e-mail to read through.

Here is another problem with holding biweekly O3s: if you miss one O3, this means you're now having *monthly* O3s. This is not good, as you'll see.

Mike Auzenne, cofounder of Manager Tools, tried holding biweekly O3s when he was an executive. Mike was working at MCI when it was acquired by WorldCom and went through bankruptcy. He had 10 directs at the time and was doing One On Ones for 30 minutes every week. He was spending five hours a week in One On Ones. Then he started getting heavily involved in the bankruptcy preparation and proceedings.

He needed time in his schedule, so he started having One On Ones biweekly in order to get five hours back every other week. He felt like things were good, that relationships were established, so his directs could tolerate having O3s every other week. Within a couple of weeks, it all fell apart. Not only did he *not* get five hours back in his schedule, but he also ended up spending more time dealing with more issues because of the lack of regular communication with his directs. When he had his One On Ones scheduled weekly, people weren't interrupting him all the time. Directs weren't always trying to get his attention. All that time in his schedule that he had gotten back, all the efficiencies, all the deeper relationships that helped make everything work smoothly just evaporated—simply by going from weekly O3s to biweekly O3s.

A caveat: if you have more than ten directs, it's okay to start with biweekly O3s. Trying to find, say, 8 hours (16 half hours for 16 directs) in your week may be a bridge too far. Spend 8 to 12 weeks allowing your schedule to absorb the 4 hours a week, and then try moving to weekly. (This habit of stressing your calendar will prepare you well for executive life, if you aspire to it.)

Furthermore, if you're reading all of this and your team is much bigger than 10 to 16 directs, our solutions will start to weaken in terms of their effectiveness. We've had some managers with as many as 30 directs included in some of our research, but we've never broken out data on teams that were bigger than 15. Anecdotally, managers who have as many as 30 directs do get better results and retention when they do One On Ones, even biweekly, or triweekly. Those results are not nearly as significant as those for managers with more "normal" spans of control.

I would argue that with a team that big, you have an organizational structure problem and not a managerial behavior problem. And, I know, that's not your fault. If you want some help thinking about team size (sorry, there's no ideal), we have some recommendations. [There's a Cast for That™.]

Monthly

We urge you *not* to have monthly One On Ones. *We have never seen an outcome where monthly O3s have improved performance.* In every instance, results and retention have stayed unchanged or have declined.

Think of it this way: suppose someone told you that she wanted to build a relationship with you and then told you, "We should be able to do it in 30 minutes, once a month." That shouldn't pass your sniff test. It doesn't make any sense to have a goal for a meeting (relationships) the frequency of which (monthly) obviates the goal.

And directs *hate* them. They tell us this all the time. They know they won't be building any relationship or any trust of any significance with you. There's no way you can give timely feedback monthly. They tell us managers end up asking for monthly reports before their O3, making it a miniature performance review or planning session rather than a two-way street.

There are hundreds of CEOs all over the world doing MTO3s. And they're doing them weekly. Sure, they miss sometimes. But they're not doing them monthly because they're "too busy." And neither should you.

30-Minute Meeting

Our data show that 30 minutes is the magic number for scheduling time for O3s. There's no benefit to going longer than 30 minutes, and going longer generally causes a reduction in "compliance." Managers who schedule O3s longer than 30 minutes mean well, but often they cancel them more frequently—so much so that directs make note of it.

You don't need more than 30 minutes—if done weekly—to get value out of your O3s. It might seem that you would, but our data say that there's not the value you might expect.

Twice when we tested 45-minute O3s, and even hour-long O3s, we got no more improvement in results and retention than we did with 30-minute O3s. On the other hand, compliance dropped: the likelihood of a meeting being canceled or being significantly shortened increased notably.

We've also tested One On Ones that were held for less than 30 minutes, and results similarly declined. There were extensive anecdotal comments about having "too little time." Both managers and directs commented that, when a 20-minute O3 started late, it was of limited value. [We know a lot of meetings start late. There's a Cast for That™.]

Regarding "compliance" (stated as a percentage, the number of O3s that you conduct versus how many were scheduled), our data show that 85 percent compliance appears to be the demarcation between getting the results you want and something less. Managers who conduct at least 85 percent of their O3s over a period of months achieve much of the results and retention improvement that managers get if they have 100 percent of their One On Ones. Once they fall below 85 percent, though, results and retention improvements are less likely. When they fall below 50 percent, it's better just to stop having O3s, in terms of the benefit (more like cost) and the time you're spending.

By studying meeting behavior, we've also learned that it's better to have a jam-packed meeting that lasts 30 minutes than to have a relaxed meeting that is scheduled for an hour but for which you only have 40 to 45 minutes' worth of content. If you overschedule a meeting, your directs will gradually begin to underprepare for them and will lose interest. Shorter, more compact, and busier 30-minute meetings will cause you and your directs to use them fully and to not miss them. Who wants another hour-long meeting that starts late and/or finishes late, which causes you to be late to your next back-to-back-to-back, hour-long meeting march?

There is one exception that I support and recommend, because I have seen it work well. If you're a senior executive, schedule O3s for an hour. One of my CEO clients (and, yes, CEOs have a role managing their directs and need One On Ones, too) told me once, "I need an hour for my One On Ones, and they're still completely full. No way could I do them for 30 minutes. I just can't finish everything we need to discuss every week with my directs." They all manage 100, 200, and 300 million USD lines of business for their firm." So the CEO client scheduled them for an hour. That made sense to me.

With Each of Your Directs

If you're going to do O3s, you've got to do them with *all of your directs*. This seems obvious, but every once in a while in our work with client managers, we hear comments such as these: "Well, I only do them with my top two people." "I do them weekly with one person and biweekly for everyone else."

This kind of selection is anathema to creating the feeling of being a team among your directs. Basically, it tells some of your directs, "You're less important than she is." While there may be a case to be made for that (one of your directs may have a special role), that's usually not the way directs see it.

If you do have a special case for one or two directs, there's nothing wrong with spending more time with them than with other team members. *Just do it at a time other than your One On One.* Schedule a special one-hour meeting with those one or two directs to discuss projects, or issues, or whatever makes their role unique. One On Ones are not about differentiating among directs but, rather, about making time for *each* direct, in order to develop a relationship with each one. Take it from an engineer: like it or not, your relationship with your directs is a force multiplier. The more you know about all of your directs—not just your top performers—the more they will trust you, and the better you will be at getting the most out of each one of them.

You should not hold One On Ones with anyone other than your direct reports. *This means that you don't do One On Ones with people who report to your directs.* (A caveat: you can do peer One On Ones with, say, other managers who report to your boss and with whom you need to maintain a strong relationship.) [There's a Cast for That™.]

We hear stories all the time from managers who are "doing biweekly O3s so that I can meet with all 20 of my directs." When we probe, we discover that they really only have four *direct* reports, and the other 16 report to their directs. Those other 16 are certainly part of the organization and are valuable, but they are not directs. When we share this with the managers, they respond that they want to "stay in touch with the folks I used to manage before I got this latest promotion." For the record, "direct" means someone who reports directly to you. It doesn't mean *anyone* in your organization.

Doing One On Ones with your "skips" is a very bad idea. ("Skips" is a large organization's term for someone who reports to one of your directs. "Directs" are the people who report *directly* to you. And "skip level" is used if you have to *skip* a level in the organizational chart to get to them.)

How DO you "stay in touch" with those in your organization who are "below" your directs? First, *insist on your subordinate managers doing One On Ones with their directs.* Your immediate subordinate managers are responsible for their relationships with their directs. The way you maintain your relationship with your skips (and even levels below that, if it applies to you) is by keeping a strong relationship with your directs *and relying on them to maintain relationships with theirs.* Any other model for this just doesn't scale.

What this means is that you won't be able to have the same relationship with people who are two or more levels down from you.

You won't, but it's okay, because you're not supposed to. Efforts to do so are a waste of your most precious resource as a manager: your time. Build an organization of effective managers under you. This is how organizations stay healthy and effective as they grow. [There's a Cast for That™.]

The Manager Takes Notes

When we teach One On Ones at our public conferences and at client sites, we often say:

If you're not taking notes, it's not a Manager Tools One On One.

One of the more surprising results of our studies of effectiveness of One On Ones was what we learned about note taking. We had assumed that, because the meeting was about "relationships," which sounds "soft" to engineers like me, there wasn't a need to take notes. We'd just . . . talk. Note taking would be detrimental to our eye contact with the direct in our discussion.

We were completely wrong. Directs have told us in every study we've ever done that their manager taking notes actually *elevates* the conversation, making it more important. Managers who just chatted but didn't take notes about possible follow-up were deemed to be less engaged, less interested, and less likely to take action on topics that came up. There was a theme: in One On Ones in which the manager did no note taking, the directs felt that the manager didn't care about what was being said from a professional perspective.

The lack of note taking added to the chance that managers and directs would talk less about work. While in some cases that was appreciated, in the majority of the cases, there was a general dislike about the lack of note taking. It made the O3 feel like a personal meeting, as *opposed to* a business meeting. The fact is, O3s are business meetings about results, and sometimes personal matters are discussed.

The problem with a One On One in which the manager does not take notes isn't the lack of note taking; it's the lack of accountability that no note taking implies.

Work *will* get done in your O3s. What other work meeting do you go to where you don't take a notebook and a pen? In our other award-winning podcast, Career Tools, one of the casts is titled, *A Notebook and a Pen* [There's A Cast For That™].

The way we recommend note taking is easy. We suggest that you get either one larger notebook with tabs separating the notes for each direct, or, if you prefer, a number of skinny notebooks, one for each direct.

We also recommend that you use a document that is easily seen to be a One-On-One form when you take notes. For most people, a little bit of structure will improve your recall. We have our standard form, and many user-submitted forms that we have tested, on our website, which you can download for free. They're in .doc format, so you can modify them to fit your style and tendencies. There are also foreign language versions of our form. Make multiple copies of your One-On-One form (O3F), to make your notebook(s) ready for your first weeks of O3s.

What you *don't* want to use to take notes is your normal "go to meeting" notebook, the one that you take with you to all of your meetings, which you refer to when you are trying to remember who said what and when they said it. If you use that notebook, all of your O3 notes will be scattered among all your other meeting notes, making preparation for your next O3 with a given direct nearly impossible. You won't be able to find what you agreed to, what the issues were, or what feedback you gave or forgot to give without leafing through many pages. (If you're getting frustrated that I'm talking about using pen and paper, and not a digital tool, please see our guidelines below about using laptops and tablets.)

There are some specific areas we recommend you pay special attention to when you take notes in each O3. We recommend that you have some distinctive way to capture deliverables. When we say *distinctive*, we mean that you can immediately see it quickly, every time, at first glance, at any O3 form on your desk.

One-On-One forms are not high level strategy documents. For every manager whose One On Ones we're familiar with, O3s tend to be very down into the details, very specific, very much about what's happening this week. Because they're that way, it would be hard to have such a meeting and not have your directs talk about the tasks and responsibilities that go with day-to-day work stuff. In addition, because One On Ones are also about relationships, trust is especially important. That means that managers have to be sure to do what they say they're going to do. Thus, remembering what we've committed to do takes on special meaning.

Circle what you promise to do, underline what you promise to do, or put asterisks next to what you promise to do, but be able to see your deliverables—your promises—at a glance.

We recommend that you capture communications or responsibilities in a *different* way. We apply the same distinctiveness principle to any notes that require us to engage in any form of communication, with anyone. These could probably be classified as deliverables as well, but we and others have found that making the distinction is helpful. Maybe you would use a rectangle or a double underline.

We recommend that you capture feedback (which we'll talk about later), but not in detail or perfectly. You want to keep track because you're obligated to keep track of your directs' performance. In some severe cases, you'll want to have notes of your performance communications with someone who is at risk of being disciplined or terminated.

Despite what most managers know or will tell you, the standard for what constitutes "documentation" is incredibly low. You don't need great details either for memory or for official record keeping when it comes to feedback. You don't need long memorandum for record (MFRs) that summarize your legal case. You need the raw data that will allow HR and their lawyers to construct a history of you communicating frequently with your directs about their performance. The key to this documentation isn't form, or formality, or length. It is whether or not it is "contemporaneous," that is, documented roughly at the same time as the incident or communication.

Whatever technique, form, or style you use to capture the feedback you've given, it ought to be easily visible and immediately obvious to you. I use a capital *F* with a plus or a minus next to it, and the recipient's first initial, with usually some indication of what the feedback was about. There might be an arrow to another part of the form, to another note. There could be a number next to the F− or F+ indicating number of instances of feedback at that time.

This is all the formality that your HR or legal department needs. You don't need to meet some legal standard, write a memo, or write out exactly what you said or how your directs responded. Note taking is a much sturdier art form than that. It's unlikely you'll need raw recall of some obscure note 18 months later. Shorter times allow us to keep some semblance of context, and the barest of basics will serve well enough. Here are two examples:

F+, W, CT perf. Improved (I gave positive feedback to Wendii, one of my directs, for the improvement in Career Tools podcast listening stats.)

F+, M, 1MM sales. (I gave positive feedback to Maggie, who works for me, for achieving her goal of one million USD in sales by the end of the first quarter.)

Notes such as these are quite sufficient.

Finally, we recommend that you capture coaching notes on the back of the previous week's O3 form. This is not so much a "how" to take notes recommendation but a "where" to take notes idea. One of our listeners recommended it, and we find it to be an excellent recommendation. (More on this when we discuss coaching in detail).

Rather than mixing your coaching notes with the rest of your One-On-One notes, write them on the back of the previous One-On-One form. If you use a normal notebook setup, with your weekly notes proceeding from front to back in chronological (NOT reverse chronological order), then when you open the notebook or folder, the back side of last week's form lies open to your eye to the left of this week's form's front side.

Where to Conduct One On Ones

Don't do a One On One in public. One On Ones are like feedback in the sense that they are for the private use of one individual. The One On One you're having with one of your directs is for you and that one direct.

We're not suggesting, though, that you should aim for secrecy. Public and private exist on a spectrum. There are very few things, professionally, that are done in complete privacy. Privacy implies that you've got to have an office. Our guiding principle is that you can't have a One On One in public, but you don't have to be completely private either.

You could have a completely appropriate, totally professional, not in public, yet not private One On One in the middle of the cafeteria at 10 o'clock in the morning. There's always a steady stream of people coming to the cafeteria to get coffee. You could be sitting 15 feet from the center aisle, across the table from one another, or you could be sitting next to one another, and have a meeting that is in a public space; yet it's not a public meeting, because everyone would know that you're meeting with one person, and they're not invited to come and sit down with you.

We don't recommend that you search for privacy. If you have an office, that's the perfect spot to do it. We don't recommend that you avoid your office simply because it's your office. Your directs are not afraid of your office. (If they're afraid, then they're afraid of you.) You don't have to close the door, either. Some people do so, and that's fine; you can leave the door open, and that's fine as well.

Please, don't go to the direct's office. Don't go from your office to the direct's cubicle, because one person going to 6 or 7 or 10 different places doesn't make any sense. It's much smarter to have six or seven or 10 people come to one place, and, frankly, it makes it much easier on you. You have multiple meetings like this; they only have one. The logistics of getting away from your desk and out of your office, and finding your directs gets in the way of your work and just puts another hurdle, or barrier, between you and the One On One.

If you have a cubicle, it's probably completely fine as a space in which to conduct a One On One. When we're thinking "cubicle," we're thinking of a three-sided work space in which you have a desk, usually your computer in the corner of the desk, and often a keyboard tray. Here's our rule about using your cubicle to conduct a One On One: if you can measure your cubicle, and it's six feet wide or less, and the walls are only 6 to 12 inches higher than the desk, then those really aren't walls. If you have walls that are higher than that, and the width of your cubicle is more than six feet, you can do a One On One in your cubicle. Ask your direct to bring a chair over, if you have an extra chair or a folding chair, and have the direct place it next to you, scoot over a little bit, lower your voice, and have a quiet conversation.

You may be reading this and thinking, "Well, that's not ideal." And you're right. I recommend it, however, because it's a reasonable solution based on the situation many managers face. Don't make the perfect the enemy of the good. Directs *do not* need total privacy behind closed doors to develop a great professional relationship with you.

If you're having a quiet conversation, there's usually enough ambient noise in most workplaces so that you can have a private conversation that will be masked by the ambient noise (e.g., the sound of keyboards, printers, and fax machines; people moving around; the hum of air conditioning; etc.).

You can have One On Ones for one, two, three, four, or five months in your cubicle and gradually build up enough trust so that your directs will feel they can share with you something personal or embarrassing, something they're worried about—maybe about family, health, or sickness—or a fear about the organization. At that point, if they really need a space that is more private than your cubicle, they'll ask for it.

5

Common Questions and Resistance to One On Ones

The Most Common Forms of One-On-One Pushback

If an initiative is important to you, it's worth thinking through the possible rejoinders and being prepared to address them. If you're not willing to verbally joust through some turbulence when you introduce a new idea, it's probably not worth doing.

First, let's be clear about pushback in general. Don't ever be surprised by it. Just because you think what you're going to try is a good idea doesn't mean that your directs will go along with it. Quite the contrary: when you change how you manage, then fear, uncertainty, and doubt (FUD) about the change are always part of the response. Don't assume it's just you; it happens to all of us.

The fact is, your directs don't respond precisely to *you* but, rather, to their perception of you. When you look in the mirror, you see the trustworthy, hardworking, well-intentioned you. You see a nice person. But, unfortunately, *your directs do not see you as a nice person*. They see you *as their boss*. This doesn't mean you are not a nice person. Of course you are. It just means that your directs don't *see you* that way. They see you first as their boss, who is also a nice person. Everything you do is seen through the lens of your role power and a reasonable fear of what that power could mean for them, their career, and their family. The fact that you would never do any of the things they worry you might do (because a previous boss actually did them) is irrelevant. What matters to them is that *you can*, and they would be foolish not to consider this in their relationship with you.

So, the fear your role power engenders creates an initial negative response to new managerial behaviors. It's normal when it happens. Having a response to some of the most likely objections will improve the speed of your implementation and the breadth of support from your directs.

The three most common forms of pushback against O3s are the following:

1. It's micromanaging.
2. I don't have time.
3. We talk all the time (which we've covered previously).

It's Micromanaging

Some directs think One On Ones are "micromanaging." They don't need them, they don't like them, and they don't want them.

Before we tell you how to answer this negative response, keep in mind a likely truth about your own situation: would you deny YOUR boss the right to see you for 30 minutes once a week? Would you turn down his request for a meeting? Would you just not go?

Think about it. Your boss says she has a new way of doing budgeting that is better and faster. Are you going to tell her no? She says, "We're changing the way we do our expense reporting, so we will have to learn a new way, but it will be worth it." Are you going to go over her head to complain? The company has a new budget process, a new annual review, a new vacation policy, a new expense reporting software, a new mobile phone contract, a new vendor for shipping. Are you really going to ignore the company's policies? Of course you're not.

Never tolerate from your directs what you would not do to your boss.

Okay, but how should you answer the accusation that One On Ones are micromanaging?

First of all, One On Ones are not micromanaging. That's ludicrous. From the company's perspective (which is the perspective the manager must take), a direct who wishes for virtually no managerial oversight is a liability risk.

The direct who believes that a 30-minute meeting once a week is burdensome and means that you are overbearing is telling you either that he is afraid of oversight, which legally is scary, or that he is above it, which is a level of arrogance that could tear apart your team.

The problem today with the average manager-direct relationship is NOT one of too much management but of far too little. Management, reasonably practiced, in virtually every organization, provides necessary guidance, controls, and incentives far below a level that is intrusive or detrimental.

The ultimate defense of O3s is a reminder of what micromanagement REALLY is. Here's the Manager Tools' definition of micromanagement:

Micromanagement is the systemic and routine application of an intrusive relationship such that the manager assigns a task, explains what to do, how to do it, insists on total process compliance, and then observes the work in real time, correcting the work as it is being done, and, in the event of divergence from standards, taking OVER the work and completing it himself.

A demanding boss is *not* a micromanager. Asking for reports is *not* micromanaging. Expecting updates is *not* micromanaging. Asking for one meeting a week is *not* micromanaging someone. Spending time communicating about tasks, deliverables, deadlines, successes, failures, growth opportunities, and, yes, even family—is *not* micromanaging in any way.

So, when one of your directs accuses you mistakenly of trying to micromanage her, address it head-on. Here's what you say, in a calm and relaxed voice:

"One On Ones are really pretty far from micromanagement, that to compare them is to show that we've got really different ideas about what each of them are, and what they mean. Micromanagement is the systemic and routine application of an intrusive relationship such that the manager assigns a task, explains what to do, how to do it, insists on total process compliance, and then observes the work in real time, correcting the work as it is being done, and, in the event of divergence from standards, taking OVER the work and completing it himself.

"A One On One, on the other hand, is a 30-minute meeting, held once a week, between you and me. That's it. There's a very brief agenda, no reporting is required, and you will need only about two to three minutes of preparation time each week. I really don't see One On Ones as being anywhere near micromanagement."

Micromanagement is by definition unreasonable. One On Ones are not unreasonable, and the reason they're not is that they basically are a new form of communication that eliminates several other less efficient and less effective forms of communication, such as waiting in line to see the boss, 10 three-minute conversations versus one 15-minute conversation about 10 different things, more frequent feedback, more timely feedback, an opportunity to receive coaching, a reduction in e-mail miscommunications, and steady communications despite an excessively high (or low) operational tempo.

What manager who considers herself effective would argue that she does *not* do these things: talk about performance, answer questions, provide feedback, assign work, praise, provide coaching, talk about relationships, discuss development, develop relationships, inquire about the status of assigned tasks, expect status reporting, pay attention to work-family balance, plan, check the work of others, and reward.

These are the things done in One On Ones. Would someone seriously argue that all of the above getting done at one time—more efficiently and more regularly for the direct, and definitely more efficiently for the manager—as opposed to having 20 conversations throughout the week, many often inconclusive due to time constraints—is somehow bad, inefficient, or ineffective?

Further, One On Ones can't be micromanaging if you're only asking for only 1 percent—1 percent!—of a direct's time. Why is it 1 percent? Simple math: if your direct works 50 hours a week, one half-hour of that is 1/100th of their time each week, month, and year.

The idea that 1/100th of a direct's time cannot be spent in work-related meetings with his boss because it would be too intrusive is laughable.

Finally, the answer to a direct who pushes back on O3s because they are micromanagement is simply to insist on having them. While we at Manager Tools know that relationship power is the clear Number 1 of the three types of power, we never said that it was the only way to influence. Sometimes, using your role power is necessary. Remember, though, when you DO use your role power, it is always more effective if it rests on a strong foundation of a trusting relationship. Role power is *heightened by* stronger relationships with one's team.

After telling your directs why O3s aren't micromanaging, you can also say, "I hear your input, and I've decided to move forward. I look forward to starting the process."

I Don't Have Time

The second most common pushback is from directs who say they don't have time for One On Ones because they're too busy.

When your directs tell you they're too busy, they're talking about how busy they are *right now*. It's true in a lot of organizations (though in many organizations, it's claimed to be true but actually isn't). But, if we allowed every new idea to be compared to everyone's current schedule, almost no one would introduce new ideas to change or improve performance, behavior, quality, quantity, or efficiency.

That's why, when we announce that we're going to start doing One On Ones, we announce that they won't start for three weeks. Part of that is to allow for the scheduling to take place. It takes a day or two for directs to pick their times. Another part of that is to allow time to answer questions. There are always questions when you change how you manage others. Part of the lag is also to allow us time to brief everyone, together, which may take a couple of days to set up. In addition, it allows directs who are so inclined to listen to or read the guidance you might make available to them. (We will discuss this further in Chapter 6.)

But the main reason for the three-week lag time is that people who have full calendars the week of the announcement rarely will have that same fullness three weeks from now. Our calendars (look at your own for validation) tend to fill up in a rolling three-to-five-day wave of requests and acceptances. If you're a busy person, today is almost always as full as you can get it. Tomorrow is probably also full. Five days from now, however, we'd wager that your calendar is somewhat less filled. Maybe 50 percent? And three weeks from now there likely is virtually nothing on it except perhaps two to three standing weekly meetings. They probably represent less than 10 percent of your total available time that week.

So, when your directs object on the basis of being too busy, tell them that you know and respect that, and that's why you're scheduling the One On Ones now for three weeks from now—when you know they have nothing already scheduled.

Here's how it might sound in an actual exchange:

Direct: I don't have time for another meeting. I'm swamped with work. You know that.

Manager: I know you're busy right now. Thanks for the hard work. I appreciate it and respect it. And that's why I'm not asking you to start now. I'm asking for time on your calendar three weeks from now. I checked, and there's nothing on your calendar then.

Direct: But by then I will have stuff on my calendar. It always fills up. I'm always busy.

Manager: Yes, but when it starts filling up a few days before our first scheduled One On One, what fills up your calendar will have one less half hour to work with. That's not too much to ask.

If it helps, another approach you can take to combat the "busy" pushback is that, if your directs are all so busy that they don't have time for anything more, they better get their priorities straight. They may well be *so* busy that they're not making time for the truly critical issues and opportunities. They need to be aligned, and what better way than a regular check-in?

"Busyness" is one of the most frequently used defenses against manager initiatives: "I don't have time. I'm too busy. What do you want me NOT to do in order to have time to do this new thing?"

The defensiveness that our directs feel is reasonable. Nevertheless, being so busy that one can't change has dangerous implications. As busy as everyone is, this defense, left unanswered, suggests that the organization will never change. Yet, we all know that the busiest and most successful organizations change all the time. How do they change and get better when they are busy, too, just like we are? How can our busyness justify NOT changing, when they change when they're busy and still deliver results?

The answer, of course, is that busyness is no defense of anything. By definition, everyone's supposed to be "busy" or at least fully using their skills. (In fact, organizational behavior experts tell us that those people who probably don't have enough to do still fill up their hours. And they, too, not surprisingly, describe themselves as "busy.")

Let's look at "busyness" a different way. Being busy to most people means they're working hard all day, every day, at work. "Busy" can be slightly different from "I'm in meetings all the time." "Busy" includes all the work one has to accomplish, in addition to all the time spent in meetings. But, at its core, "busy" means, "I have more work to do than I have time to do it." Put differently, you're busy if you're not getting all your work done. Just ask yourself: do you feel busy? And then, do you go home every night with all your work having been done?

When a direct says he doesn't have time to attend One On Ones, it's a sign that he is fully busy, with work he's not getting done. But if this is a defense against a new obligation, then you're never going to get that direct to ever do anything new.

There's a simple rule about work when there's more than can be done: **Before trying to get more of everything done, get the most important things done first.** This is a simple argument that it's better to try to first achieve results through *effectiveness*—doing the right things, the valuable things, the important things—before trying to achieve results through *efficiency*—doing the same work in less time. Work on the right things first. Then become more efficient at doing those right things, and you'll have more time for either more right things or some less important things.

So, when a direct says she doesn't have time or is too busy for One On Ones, another effective response is to explain to her that, if she's so busy, you both know that she's not getting everything done, which means you need to make sure that she's working on the right things first and foremost. And that means talking more about what she's working on, to achieve alignment, through the One On One.

Here's how it might sound in an actual exchange:

Direct: I'm too busy for another (worthless) meeting. I've already got too much to do and not enough time to do it. How is (yet) another meeting going to help me with that?

Manager: I know you're busy. We're all busy. And, as an aside, having too much work to do doesn't stop the VPs and directors from asking us to hold an extra meeting or two. But anyway, look, if you're that busy, we'd better be sure that you're working on the right things. My guess is that there are things you're working on that I don't know about, and, if you're like me, there are also some things that you're working on that you like doing but that maybe aren't the best for the team or the organization. No offense. So, if there's more work than you can do, we've absolutely got to be sure that whatever you're doing is the most important. And seriously, a half-hour meeting—about 1 percent of your work week—isn't going to make your workload any worse.

I assure you that, when you get some alignment out of your directs, you'll get more time back in your week than you spend in your One On Ones. Guaranteed.

Finally, probably the easiest response to give to a direct who has no time for One On Ones is to show her how little time you're asking for. Part of the reason this response works is because so few people think globally or strategically about their time and calendar/schedule. They think about the now, and the near-term, usually in the form of impending deadlines. Most approaches to creating more time are about spending fewer minutes on each of the next few things they're working on.

This approach is tactical. It might garner some saved time, but it will be incremental. The highly effective approach is to apportion one's time differently, by starting from the top down. *Getting Things Done* by David Allen teaches this beautifully. The book *168 Hours* by Laura Vanderkam does it very well. The concept is also beautifully illustrated in a widely quoted story called "The Big Rocks" by Stephen Covey.

When you're working in "the now," and someone asks for half an hour of your time, apoplexy might be a reasonable response. You never feel like you have half an hour when you're up against the deadlines of "the now." Yet, if I asked you for 30 minutes of your time next month, you'd surely be able to make that work.

Let's do the math for a whole year of One On Ones: 30 minutes a week times 52 weeks. Wait, that's not entirely accurate. It should be 30 minutes for 52 weeks, minus two weeks of vacation for you and minus two weeks of vacation for your direct. So, now we have 30 minutes times 48 weeks. That gives us 24 hours. If we assume eight-hour workdays, that's three days every year.

The right response to our math might be, "Are you kidding me? My directs don't have a measly three days *in an entire year* to meet with me to talk about work, their performance and development, and any other thing they would like to talk about? When our website talks about team players and communication and collaboration? Inconceivable! And I think that word means exactly what I think it means."

If we're really going to get snarky, people are always claiming that they're working 50-hour weeks (and more). So, now we're only talking about *two days a year!* Inconceivable.

Furthermore, the directs only have to talk for 15 of those 30 minutes, which means we're asking them to come talk to us *one day a year*.

The idea that someone doesn't have this much time in a year is preposterous. Here's how it might sound in an actual exchange:

Direct: I just don't have time for this, boss. You've given me tons to do, and I can feel the tension at home, too, with the hours I'm spending.

Manager: Okay, well, first things first. If there are problems at home with your hours, let's talk about that. Family first—go home, darn it.

And look, I'm not asking for much time. It's kind of silly for us to have a conversation about what amounts to two to three workdays in an entire year being too much to handle. In a 50-hour week, 30 minutes is 1 percent of your week. You're going to struggle to convince me that you can't spare that much time for open communication when your calendar three weeks from now is so open? So, let's start.

One final response to the pushback would be simply to insist, again, using role power. We don't recommend that you do this very often. We always start with relationship power. There are three forms of power or influence in organizations. Role power, that which the organization grants you to compel others to act for the organization; relationship power, your own ability to change behaviors of others because of their knowledge of, and trust in, you; and expertise power, others' perception of your technical, industrial, or topical knowledge that causes them to follow your guidance.

Just because we know that relationship power is the ultimate lever, this doesn't mean that role power doesn't exist. If we use it rarely, when we do use it, we will be respected. Role power tends to exist in inverse proportion to how often you use it. Sometimes, to get people to overcome their objections, it's necessary for them to see the benefits of the new plan rather than for you to try to convince them of its benefits in advance.

If you've tried some or all of the other responses, it's fair to say you've made a solid effort. And, time being what it is, although we owe each of our directs a reasonable effort at communicating with them, at some point it's both ineffective and inefficient to keep trying to use our relationship power in order to persuade them.

Here's how using role power might sound in an actual exchange:

Direct: I don't see how this helps me. It's just another meeting, rather than me getting some real work done.

Manager: Fair enough. I get that I haven't convinced you. That being said, every once in a while, I get to be in charge rather than be just a collaborator. I believe that over time this will become the most valuable time we spend each week. I haven't convinced you yet, but I'm willing to bet that the results of us doing so will. So, I'm going to insist. Pick a time, do your best to stay positive, and let's behave our way into believing.

This is not our first choice for responding, but it is completely appropriate when you believe in your plans.

Talking Too Much and Talking Too Little

So, now you've got your One On Ones scheduled, and they will be held weekly for 30 minutes with each of your directs. If you're like most managers we train, the question on your mind is: "What are we going to talk about?"

Manager Tools One On Ones are business meetings. They're about building relationships, but the primary purpose of the relationships you're building is results. Since they're business meetings, they have an agenda. One On Ones are not chances "to just sit around and talk," "to get to know one another informally," or "to do a quick catch-up." Managers who try these unstructured conversations discover quickly that that kind of meeting doesn't make sense in a modern workplace. Without some basic structure to your O3s, you might as well cancel them and go back to chatting with your team members in the hallway or the breakroom.

The agenda is simple: first, 10 minutes for your direct to speak, then 10 minutes for you to speak, and then 10 minutes to talk about the future. The most important item on the agenda is "first": the key to the agenda is letting your directs go first. I shared the story earlier of our very first effort with agendas, in which we let managers go first: the results were disastrous. If you go first, *no matter how important the material is that you want to talk about,* you will not get the value out of One On Ones that we've been discussing.

The direct goes first and talks about *whatever the direct wants to talk about.* There is no agenda other than the three 10-minute segments. In the vast majority of the tens of thousands of One On Ones I've recorded or gathered data about, *the manager did not know with certainty what the direct was going to want to discuss.*

The way the O3 will actually "start" is by you making a statement or asking a question. We tried, years ago, to tell managers to say nothing and just let the direct start talking, but it was awkward, according to both the managers and the directs.

Start each O3, every time, with every direct, no matter what, with the same first question. It eliminates the need to be creative, it increases the brainpower you put into listening to the answer rather than the question, and it simplifies your work.

Ask the same question every time. Memorize it, and tell your directs, "This is the question (or statement) I'm going to start every O3 with. I don't really need an answer to it; it's just a way to turn the podium over to you." You don't need to try hard to make every O3 unique. The value of O3s isn't realized because of any single instance of an O3. What's important is the constancy of them. If you memorize your question or statement, you won't have to think about it. If your directs know it's coming every week, then they will know what to expect, and they will see it as you showing respect for their time. Some examples of questions you can ask are: "How's it going?" "How are you?" "How are things?" "Your agenda—what have you been up to? What's going on?"

For a long time I started my O3s with, "Your agenda—." The reason was that, if I wasn't careful, I would mention something, comment about something, or otherwise hijack the meeting with something that *I* wanted rather than letting my directs truly own their portion of the agenda. I did it to combat my own weakness.

Whatever you do, don't ask a question you expect a real or detailed answer to. A good example of this is a manager who is thinking, "This is a relationship meeting, so let's keep it casual, with a little bit of chit-chat to start." So a Monday One On One starts with "How was your weekend?" But now, for the first two minutes of the O3, the direct is answering your question. You've just set the agenda, and your direct is talking about what you want to talk about. Twenty percent of their time with you is taken up with *your* issues, *not* with issues of interest to *them*.

As we said, the O3 is a 30-minute meeting. You don't have time for chit-chat; that's why it's not on the agenda.

What types of things might your directs want to talk about? On one level: *who knows?* That's part of the value of the meeting. If you're going to build a relationship with someone whom you're going to trust to do high-quality work without micromanaging that person, you're going to have to respect that the person is different from you. Your directs have different joys and pains, different issues and successes at home, and different ways of thinking about their work than you do. If you never give those differences the opportunity to be voiced, you're not really trying to create a relationship.

I sometimes joke and call this portion of the meeting "puppies and rainbows," because if my direct wants to talk about puppies or rainbows—*neither of which hold the kind of fascination for me that so many others feel for them*—I'll listen. I'll ask questions. I'll take notes. If it's important to my team member, *it's important to me*. That's how you build relationships.

So, don't ask your directs for a list of topics. I understand that you don't want to be unprepared for whatever they're going to bring up.

We hear that a lot. But if you expect a list or agenda, now your direct is having to spend time coming up with that agenda each week. Further, if the direct has a tough topic to discuss with you, and you see it on the agenda and want to address it immediately, *you're doing it on your time, and very likely the direct won't be prepared when you ask the direct to talk about it before the O3.*

Also, it's not a good idea to send a direct a list of topics that you're going to talk about. In theory, this makes good sense: the direct will be prepared, and the meeting will be more efficient. What actually happens in far too many cases is that the direct will actually spend time in *their* portion of the agenda addressing *your* list. You can tell us it's not so, you really only mean to talk about your list during your time. But that's not what our years of research have shown. *It has been our experience that managers who share a list of topics in advance step on the direct's agenda, reducing the direct's satisfaction with the meeting.*

All that being said, though, we do have some data about what your directs want to talk about. Seventy-four percent of directs say that what they want to spend most of their time talking about in their One On Ones with their boss is *work*. And why not? It's the primary link between you and your directs. Do you sit around thinking that, if your boss started having O3s with you, you'd use that time to have rambling conversations about nothing important? Of course not.

A typical O3 direct's portion includes updates about ongoing work, questions about problems they're having, project status reports, requests for assistance with budgets or communications, requests for guidance about next steps or about approaching a problem, verification of rumors they've heard, clarification of what you want or how you want something done, notifications of tasks they've finished, follow-up on pending actions, reminders of information or materials they need from you, and so on.

If your O3s go like this, and you become worried that they're "too much like status updates" *stop worrying*. What you're getting from your directs is normal for many directs. This is not true for *all* directs: some will share more personal information than others. Some will lead with it (but only a small minority, and only occasionally). Mostly, your O3s will be about work.

From your direct's perspective, the reason it's a valuable "work" discussion is because it's about *their* work during their portion of the agenda—not what they do for your work and your agenda (though clearly they're related), but their work.

Are One On Ones personal or work related? One On Ones create a forum for both. Trust your directs to choose to talk about what's important to them.

During *your* 10 minutes, you, too, get to talk about whatever you want. While 74 percent of directs say that what they most want to talk about is work, 89 *percent of managers* say they want to talk about work. So, probably you will ask for updates on ongoing work, assign new work, ask about problems with existing work, plan for upcoming work, and share ideas for potential new work. That makes you normal.

Can you talk about personal things yourself? Yes. You can mention your family if you like, but you don't have to. You can share something about your weekend if you like. You can talk about volunteer work you're doing, television shows or movies that you've recently seen, parties you went to, chores you did, or the weather you're experiencing. These would be normal conversational topics in any normal relationship, so they're all okay.

But you'll probably talk about work, and that's just fine.

If you want more guidance about work and personal topics in One On Ones, There's a Cast for That™.

There is one exception to you talking about whatever you'd like in your portion of your MTO3. As a general rule, if there's any information that you need to get out to your entire team, we recommend that it go out in what we would call a "waterfall meeting," not in your One On Ones. This is likely to be your weekly staff meeting [There's a Cast for That™], where you will only have to say it once, to *all* of your directs at the same time, rather than seven times—once to *each* of your directs. Plus, if you share it individually, you'll get many of the same questions repeated, and you'll end up giving different answers. All of this is terribly inefficient. Don't use your O3s to pass down standard information that everyone's getting.

The last 10 minutes of your O3s give you an opportunity, *periodically*, to talk about the future. You probably will only have time to do so once every 20 sessions, because, as we'll discuss, 30 minutes probably isn't long enough to cover everything that you and your direct want to cover. Discussing big-picture or future plans with your directs two to three times a year is probably about right.

The 10/10/10 agenda is a template; you are not required to discuss the big picture or the future every week.

An agenda that would be more representative of how One On Ones actually occur would be 15/15: the direct speaks first, and then you speak. When we first started teaching O3s, we got some interesting feedback. Many managers shared two common themes in their comments: (1) *Sometimes we run short; what should I do?* (2) *I'm way more down in the weeds than I used to be, which is great, but I'd love to have some big-picture discussions every once in a while.*

The answer to the first question is easy: *when you're done, you're done.* If an O3's content runs out, you're done. Lucky you; you get some time back in your day.

Because we heard about the lack of big-picture discussions and running short occasionally, we simply combined the two problems into one solution. The last 10 minutes on the agenda is a *reminder* to cover the future or big picture when you think the timing is reasonable and you run short. If you don't run short, don't cover the future. If you run short two weeks in a row, there is no need to cover the future all over again (unless there are worthy issues to discuss) so soon.

At this point, you may be wondering about how most O3s go relative to the agenda. The average direct talks for 21 minutes. It would follow that we would then say that managers get the final nine minutes, but that's not exactly true, because managers report that they often run over the scheduled time allotted for the meeting, in order to cover their list of items.

What should you do, though, about directs who talk too little? Wouldn't that be awkward? What's interesting about this is the assumption that directs who talk too little will be your biggest problem. Just the opposite is true: directs are far more likely to talk too much than too little. We surveyed several hundred managers about the loquacity of their directs, and they told us that roughly 65 percent of their directs "talk about the right amount," 30 percent "talk too much," and only 5 percent "talk too little."

The problem that you likely will face is directs who talk way too much, not those who clam up. Let's walk through how to handle both situations.

If a direct talks too much, start by realizing that you have an embarrassment of riches. Even if the direct takes the full 30 minutes each week for perhaps several weeks, don't overreact. Think of changing the direct's behavior as a process, to unfold slowly.

Don't practice what we call "agenda fascism." [There's a Cast for That™.] Agenda fascism means you've just told your directs that you want to spend time with them and get to know them, you tell them the meeting is for them, and you share that the agenda is 10/10/10. Then, exactly 10 minutes into the first meeting, you say, "OK, time's up. I have to cut you off."

Unfortunately, that's probably not very conducive to building a relationship with your directs. Some of you might be thinking, "Well, but if that's the agenda, we should stick to it—right?" Well, no. If that's the case, why don't all your meetings have agendas, start on time, and end on time? The agenda of a meeting always serves the purpose of the meeting, not the other way around. The agenda is there to facilitate the purpose. If the agenda is getting in the way of the purpose, you jettison the agenda to get to the purpose.

If you cut a direct off and the direct still has more to share with you, within reason, what you're doing is putting the agenda ahead of the purpose.

So, in the beginning, let your direct continue to talk. Don't worry about your list or your agenda. You can always seek your direct out later with your topics: If you ask the direct, "Got a second?" I bet the answer will be yes.

Maybe the direct is still talking after 15 minutes, or 20 minutes, or 25 minutes, or even 30 minutes. Let the direct talk. If, during every O3 for the first *month* of O3s, the direct talks for the full 30 minutes, let that happen.

After two months, you can say, "OK, I'm going to give you a reminder at 20 minutes. You've been taking the full 30 minutes, and that was fine when we were starting up, but I have my own items to cover." For the next month, you remind them at 20 minutes. This is not a hard stop, just a reminder: "Hey, it's been 20 minutes."

After another month of giving a "verbal yield sign" at 20 minutes, you can start giving a hard stop at 20 minutes: "Hey, listen, for the last month, I've been reminding you when you've gotten to 20 minutes. But now the reminder that's been a yield sign is going to become a stop sign. I really want to be able to get through my items as well."

Maybe the first time you cut the direct off will be a little awkward. After that, the direct will be fine. We've tested this with about 50 managers. It worked well, according to both managers and directs tested.

Now we come to the situation that is rarer and more difficult: the uncommunicative direct. This type of team member comes to your first One On One and basically says nothing. When you ask the person what's going on, he will say, "Nothing." When you ask how the person is doing, he will say, "Fine."

What to do? First, don't try to guess at your direct's attitude or intent. We'll talk more about this when we get to performance communications, but for now, try to focus only on their behavior: not communicating.

Our guideline is to give that team member time. Remember that every direct brings to the relationship with you, the boss, all of his previous relationships with his previous bosses. If the team member had a boss (or two) who was unethical or abusive, don't be surprised if that team member answers your request for dialogue and a relationship with silence. Don't punish him for not opening up. Don't be rude or demand. Ask for input, and if the direct has none, move on to your portion of the O3. Speak about your 10 to 20 minutes' worth of topics, and perhaps something about the future, and you're done. It's not great, but it's useful for you.

If the pattern continues, we recommend that you ask *three times* at the start of each One On One something like this:

Manager: Whaddaya got?
Direct: Nothing.
Manager: Well, okay. Understand, this is *your* O3, and this is your portion of it. This is your 15 minutes. It's for brainstorming, asking for help, questions, discussions, sharing—whatever you want to talk about.
Direct: I'm good.
Manager: Okay. I just want to make sure you don't have anything. I have some stuff, but you get to go first. Final answer?
Direct: Nope.

You've tried three times—any more will just be annoying. So now you move on to your agenda items. Once you start realizing (after two to three weeks of silence) that there's a problem, we recommend that you start asking more questions about work status, progress, issues, concerns, and needs.

It might sound like this:

Manager: Okay, then. My turn. Hey, I noticed in the staff meeting that you were having some challenges on Project A. There was a deliverable you were going to miss. Tell me more about that. (This is said in a pleasant tone, smiling, making eye contact. You're not trying to unearth a failure, just trying to find out if help is needed.)

Direct: I'm waiting on Keith. I can't do my stuff without the stuff he owes me.

Manager: Great. When are you going to get it?

Direct: I don't know. I haven't gotten it yet.

Manager: What's your plan?

Direct: I don't know.

Manager: Have you followed up at all?

Direct: Yes.

Manager: How?

Direct: I sent Keith another e-mail.

Manager: Okay, but I've had a lot better experience getting stuff from Keith with a phone call. That's especially true since your e-mails apparently aren't working . . ."

That's how you try hard to make your One On One with a noncommunicative direct more useful.

The fact is, though, that this level of resistance is rare. I've never experienced it; neither have most of my friends and colleagues. But it does happen. Give it time, and your direct will gradually open up, over time.

Pushback on Note Taking

There are two types of pushback on note taking: managers who prefer to take notes on their laptop, and directs who are worried that the manager's notes are a form of "documentation."

We don't recommend that you take notes on your laptop, and neither does almost anyone else. Just do a quick Google search of the effectiveness of handwritten versus typed notes, and you'll agree with us. Remember as you do so that your brain stores pictures, not text. The ability to search text on your laptop or other device isn't used as often as most folks who type notes plan to, and it is much harder to remember what you typed versus what you wrote by hand.

And whether we like it or not, directs tell us that when they can see your screen, you've got your mail client running on it, and your instant messaging software. They know you're distracted by your laptop.

Plus, with a camera in your phone, you can take a picture of your handwritten notes, and now they're in your system.

That being said, we love using technology to make our lives simpler, too. If you're drawn to that, the best solutions in 2016 are to use Microsoft One Note on a tablet computer or an Apple iPad with an Apple Pencil. And you don't have to carry around a notebook (at least for O3s).

"Documentation"

When directs ask about documentation, as if it is something to be feared, the conversations we end up having with them are made much harder. What directs mean is that they fear that when their manager starts writing things down, the manager is thinking that things could become bad enough to justify some sort of disciplinary action that could require formal notes, history, and documentation.

Documentation is an obligation, not something to be feared. Every note you take, every e-mail you send, and every spreadsheet you create are all a documentation of something.

Documentation has gotten a bad name, just like annual reviews have, for stupid reasons. Annual performance reviews are a good example of how managers have lost the argument about what management is or what managers do. Annual reviews exist to allow the organization to do succession planning. They are intended to be forward-looking exercises and documents. However, because managers don't do well giving feedback, organizations (and managers) have allowed them to be co-opted into an annual feedback exercise. This is, of course, ludicrous, because annual reviews and feedback cannot modify one another reasonably.

So, if one of your directs asks, "Are you documenting this?" we recommend that you say something like the following: "Yes. But not because you're in trouble in any way. *Documenting* isn't a bad word. I don't "start documenting" when something becomes a problem. I take notes about almost everything I'm doing. If you're my top performer, I take notes about your successes. I take notes to help me remember, to allow me to refer back to something, and to be accurate. All professionals take notes all the time. The combination of my notes, my e-mails, and my work products are all forms of documentation."

Can I Do One On Ones over the Phone?

You can get great benefits from doing One On Ones over the phone. If you and your direct are not collocated, or one of you is traveling, One On Ones over the phone work very well. Our data show that you can get roughly 80 percent of the value from a phone O3 that you get from a face-to-face O3. The reason for the decline isn't the phone O3 itself; it's the distance.

I have had an average of five directs for the past 10 years, and because of my travel schedule, I have done fewer than 20 O3s face-to-face. Think about that—that's 10 years of O3s, times, say, 50 weeks a year, times five directs. That's 2,500 O3s—less than 1 percent face-to-face O3s, due to my travel schedule. If telephonic One On Ones didn't work, I wouldn't do them.

The following are some basic guidelines.

Do Phone O3s When You Can't Do Face-to-face O3s

If you CAN do face-to-face One On Ones, we recommend, of course, that you do so. The majority of managers ARE collocated with their directs, even though, more than ever, the workplace is becoming more virtual.

There are only TWO times to do phone O3s: (1) when your direct is not collocated with you, and (2) when a normally collocated direct is traveling or a manager is traveling, and a face-to-face O3 is not possible. The guidelines we suggest here apply to either of those One On Ones.

The concept is simple. Your directs are your directs, whether they are in your office location or not. If the purpose of an O3 is to encourage effective relationships, why would your relative locations change that? If we see this as a purpose and value discussion, as opposed to a form or process discussion, it's a no-brainer. The relationship you are obligated to build with your directs isn't predicated on distance, or the lack thereof. So, if you're distant from any of your directs, whether temporarily or permanently, do your O3s over the phone. Using a cell phone is fine; Skype is fine also.

Webcams Are Even Better

Webcams are better than phones in the same way that face-to-face O3s are better than phone O3s, and phone is better than nothing at all. If you and your direct have access to a webcam, use it. If you're wondering whether it will be an invasion of your direct's privacy somehow, consider this: there are Fortune 100 firms that are now requiring live webcams of all telecommuting employees. It's not an invasion of privacy. It offers a way to get a richer stream of information to help managers build a better relationship with their directs.

The Basics Still Apply

We've touched on the tools we're going to use for a phone O3, but let's remember the purpose. The phone is a tool, and the purpose of using it is to build relationships. So all those boring concepts that really have solid underpinnings still apply with regard to phone O3s:

Primary Focus on the Team Member

Regularly Scheduled

Never Missed

30 Minutes (and the 10/10/10 rule)

Take Notes

It Works Better If We Call Them

Over the years, we've tried both calling the direct and having the direct call us. Some managers say, "Well, if it's their meeting, if it's so valuable to them, then they ought to be willing to call me." Okay, but that's a bit misleading. The One On One meeting *is about them*, but it's also for both of you. Their review at the end of the year is for them, but it's done by you. Feedback is for them, but you deliver it.

If you rely on your directs to call you, you'll end up with less frequent meetings, in our experience. They get busy. We've found that managers who are expecting a call from a direct but don't get the call assume that something came up, so the managers use the time in a different way. However, when managers don't make the call to their directs, the directs assume they've been blown off by their manager because more important things came up. And believe it or not, you have more control over your calendars than your directs do, so it's easier for you to initiate the call.

If you really believe in the relationship value of One On Ones, you will make the time to call your directs, just like when you are going to a meeting in a conference room. Don't make your directs come and find you.

More Document Sharing Is Necessary

This is the biggest conclusion we've drawn for those directs who are not collocated, and it has two important purposes. The first has to do with behavior, and the second with meeting efficiency.

When it comes to managing your distant direct, you won't have as much information to go on. You won't have as many opportunities to observe their facial expressions, or their body language. The most important thing you'll be evaluating from your distant directs is their work product. What form does work product most often take in these situations? Documents.

Distance management requires that you become much more effective at managing others based on their work product. Effective managers ask for more documents from their directs in advance of phone One On Ones to give themselves a better opportunity to assess the quality and quantity of their directs' work product and to allow time to give them feedback on it.

Another reason to encourage document communications in advance is the simple one of efficiency. We've found that asking for key documents in advance speeds up the One On One. Since time is limited, efficiency increases effectiveness directly. I've spent many precious minutes of my time in a One On One looking for, waiting for, or discussing in absentia, a particular document—all for naught.

Ideally, rather than asking for documents in advance, you've created some sort of e-storage solution for your directs' work product. As a general rule, effective managers don't allow directs to keep large amounts of work product documents in storage locations that the manager can't get at without the direct's involvement.

Think of it this way: I'm your direct. We're collocated. I'm in your office for an O3. I ask you a question about a presentation, but I don't have the slide deck with me. Wouldn't you ask me to go back to my desk and get it, and we could make changes right away? Of course you would.

So, if I'm one of your distant directs, why should the distance keep us from being able to review documents? Would you allow me to say, "I can't show it to you, it's on my laptop and it's not with me?" Of course you wouldn't.

Know where your directs' work product documents are, and have them available to you both when doing a One On One.

Interruptions Are More Frequent Without Focus

We've learned this the hard way. People mistakenly believe that phone One On Ones are somehow less important than face-to-face meetings. You will be interrupted much more frequently when you're in a phone One On One than in a face-to-face One On One.

This means you have to focus. We have several suggestions for how to do this.

1. *Start with Your Back Turned.* Too many managers look out over where their directs sit when they are on the phone. Don't do this. Turn your back on the world. Close your door. Don't look around.
2. *Ignore Interruptions.* No one is ever interrupted "by someone else." Every interruption is caused by the person *being interrupted*, when that person stops what she's doing. When someone approaches, turn your back. If the person speaks to you, smile and point to the phone. If the person is standing there, waiting for you to get off the phone, turn your back. If the person touches your shoulder, hold up a hand while *not* turning around.
3. *Focus.* Stop checking your e-mails. Stop looking at the stuff on your desk. Close your eyes, and visualize your direct speaking. Shut down your browser. Quit other programs. It's only 30 minutes of your time, once a week. Your directs have earned it.

Can I Be Friends with My Directs?

You Cannot Be Friends with Your Directs

I'm really sorry to be the bearer of this bad news. Before you get frustrated, follow our logic, and you'll come to the same conclusion we have.

You might think of yourself as the boss sometimes and as your directs' friend at other times, but this kind of role switching is simply not practicable. Further, even if we ignore the friendship aspect for a moment, the appearance of friendship (whose moral obligations are always assumed) is a significant detractor to one's ability to lead and manage others.

I'll address the appearance of friendship with your team in a moment, but consider this: your boss (who speaks for the organization) will question your decisions and professionalism if he believes you have formed friendships with your directs. More senior bosses will probably go further and say, "I don't even need to think of a particular situation in order to have a concern. The fact that you don't see the potential conflicts of interest makes me question your analytical skills and foresight even before I get to ask you whom you are befriending."

Let's do some thought experiments:

1. Your friend who is a direct asks you to be the godparent to his soon-to-be-born son. Because you would accept this honor (read: obligation) if you weren't his boss, because you ARE friends, you say yes. Everyone learns of this in your company, and most are generally pleased. A month later, layoffs are discussed, and you are expected to make some recommendations about your team. Will you pause at his name in light of his family situation and your specific, personal, and perhaps even religious connection to him, or, because you would never do that, will you at least let him know early about his career risk? Furthermore, how will your

"completely unbiased" decision be viewed by your peer managers when you spare your future godson's father the loss of his job?

2. Your boss asks you to make a recommendation for someone to join a task force that is high visibility and career enhancing. He says that he wants your direct, whom he knows to be your friend, to be high on your list. However, you know that your friend is considering leaving the firm within the next 90 days (he has told you this in confidence), which would be seriously damaging to the task force and to the perception of your knowledge of your team's career planning. Will you tell your boss what your friend has asked you to keep confidential? Will you not tell your boss and hurt the firm by allowing your boss to pick someone who's leaving, in order to protect the confidence? Will you hide your knowledge of your friend's plans and lie about why someone else is a better choice? If you are asked later whether you allowed your direct/friend to serve on the task force, will you admit that you knew about his plan to leave the firm, thereby damaging your now departed friend's reputation as a fair professional in your industry?

3. Your friend has just told you "confidentially" that she has accepted a new job but that she can wait up to a month to start. You knew she was looking for another job, and you had been trying to stay neutral, because you have been working on an upcoming layoff. Unfortunately, the leaks have started, and your friend says to you, "Hey, I'll take a severance package. Six months is what the last group got a couple of years ago. Put my name on the list." Will you do so, knowing that you probably wouldn't have done it if she weren't leaving? What will you say to her if she doesn't get the package? Will you tell her something different based on whether you had her on the list or not?

4. Here's a simple scenario. Your direct/friend is looking for a different job, since your industry is a bit slow. She wants a promotion and isn't likely to get one at your firm. Are you obligated to tell your boss that you know your direct/friend is

actively looking, whether or not your boss asks? You would not have known this if you were not friends.

5. Your direct/friend tells you that his wife, a banker, let slip that a competitor is within days of trying to acquire your small-ish company's corporate parent. He tells you, "You can't tell my wife I told you—you can't tell anyone. She'll know it came from me, and she will get fired!" Will you tell your boss, now that you have this information? What will it feel like if you keep quiet and your friend later lets slip to your boss that he told you it was coming? What could your boss do?

6. Here is my favorite "direct as friend" scenario. Your direct/friend asks to speak to you confidentially. (You can't in good conscience offer that, but you do anyway.) She says, "I've stolen 10,000 dollars from the company. *What should we do?*"

Friendship implies a social obligation to someone else. We can surmise this from the number of times any number of us have agreed with one person's viewpoint on a particular topic—most commonly someone else's behavior—only later to contradict ourselves by agreeing with a different friend's totally opposite take on the situation in question. We may not directly contradict ourselves, perhaps. We may not even particularly "believe" either side with whom we are agreeing at the moment. But far more tellingly on behalf of the obligations "friendship" suggest, we agree with both as a function of the friendship and then are willing to argue that we aren't agreeing with either but are simply keeping the peace.

Friendships also cause the majority of us to enter into an implicit understanding regarding the secrecy of our friends' communications with us. One of the hallmarks of friendship is, in fact, an unstated understanding that the relationship confers the ability to share some things that normally would be closely held, or withheld from others. This "friendship confidentiality" can be invoked at any time, and, what's more, invoked retroactively: "Hey, by the way, what I just said, you won't share that, right?"

Indeed, the existence of this part of a friend relationship is so inseparable from the friendship itself that if it were revoked, the very revocation—not based on the nature of the topic, but simply the revocation, irrespective of the topic—would damage the relationship. It would not be seen as a difference of opinion or a misunderstanding to have a friend say, after you have shared something you considered private, "Hey, sorry, but *that* thing you mentioned—I don't think I can keep *that* to myself." You would surely stare at your "friend" in disbelief.

With both of these ideas—social obligation and implied secrecy—friendships run afoul of a manager's professional obligations. A manager cannot expect to be treated as a professional if she at times accepts the different set of moral obligations that friendship also implies. If you're a manager, a part of you knows this. It's not a joy to talk about, but we can't just ignore the friction between our various sets of obligations.

Your Directs Don't Think of You as a Friend (First)

Up until now, we've made the case for why a manager can't ethically be friends with a direct. But there's another side of this situation to address: the direct's side.

Let's start with one of the shocking truths of managing: your directs don't think of you as a nice person. Why? Because they think of you as the boss. We're not saying you're not a nice person. You no doubt are.

Your directs think of you first as *their boss*. Those who don't, we discover, are terribly difficult to manage. How would you feel if one of your directs, who last month was a friend and peer, came up to you and said, "I can't believe you gave me this tough assignment. I thought we were friends." We suspect you'd feel a little betrayed.

We've heard it before: the manager tells us he feels that if the direct were a true friend, the direct wouldn't have challenged the manager but would have understood that the manager had obligations.

Let's take this idea to its logical extension. Not only do your directs see you first as their boss, but also everyone else sees you as your directs' boss, not as your directs' friend. When your behaviors aren't easily understood as normal manager behaviors, others in the firm will wonder why you're not effective or not reasonable. They will assume that, regardless of any previous relationship, your decisions will be based on managerial factors, not friendship. If they ever find out otherwise, you will not be taken seriously for much longer.

You Can Be Friendly with Your Directs

Hopefully, this is the gigantic loophole so many managers want it to be. You cannot be *friends with* your directs, but yes you can be *friendly with* them. You might think that the two mean the same thing, but there is a clear difference. The difference lies in what we've already talked about. Being friendly with your directs is simply a set of *behaviors*. Smiling, asking about their free time and families, being polite, starting conversations with small talk, sharing about your own life, encouraging them to join you for lunch, accepting lunch invitations, and so on—all of these are friendly behaviors. They are appreciated, respected, and often admired by those who struggle to get along well and easily with others.

Now, you might say, "Wait, these are the things friends do," and you would be right. But, to be a friend, as opposed to simply engaging in friendly behavior, one also accepts the obligation that "being a friend" means, as opposed to just behaving in a friendly way. This is the obligation that we addressed earlier. It is the obligation of friendship, not the friendly behaviors, that is the problem with managers being friends with their directs. Friendly, yes; friends, no.

You Cannot Show Favoritism with Your Friendships

We often hear undertones of favoritism when we get asked about being friends with one's directs. "My best friend used to be a peer of mine; now he works for me." "A group of us likes to go out to the same bar—just two to three of my ten directs."

When we hear these questions and comments, we certainly understand the motivation to continue enjoying a good part of your life that existed before your promotion. We'd even guess that when managers ask us about friendships, they are RARELY asking about having equally strong friendships with everyone on their team. They're thinking of those directs who are already their friends.

Let's set up a simple series of tests for the manager-direct relationship.

- You can't *be friends* with ANY of your directs.
- You CAN *behave in a friendly way* to all of your directs.
- You can't behave in a friendly way to some of your directs—even if they're not friends—without behaving similarly with all of your other directs.

The biggest problem with having differing levels of friend-ship—from actual friends to friendly behaviors to no special relationship at all—is the perception effect. Even if you genuinely aren't friends with a direct, if you then behave in a friendly way toward her while not behaving similarly with others, this will be seen as a form of friendship and will be a cause for concern. Others will question your motivations and decisions. Your credibility will suffer.

In other words, you can't use the "friendly behavior" distinction to attempt to either hide a friendship with a direct or to differentiate among your team members. It's not ethical, and it's not effective.

You Can Drink with Your Directs

You might be wondering if you can have a drink (alcohol) with your directs. It's really pretty simple when you think about it. We will give you the benefit of the doubt here and say that drinking with your directs is NOT exclusively done just with friends but, rather, is a friendly behavior. We happen to think, based on the questions we get, that drinking IS done among friends. The moment we stipulate that, however, we would need to eliminate all drinking with all directs or come up with every possible reasonable exception. That kind of guidance is untenable.

If drinking is only a friendly behavior, then yes, you can imbibe with your directs. But remember: you can't show favoritism. If you're drinking with a smaller subset of your team regularly, you're either admitting they're your friends, or, if you wish to claim it's only friendly behavior, then the subset makes it friendly behavior that is unevenly applied. Thus, favoritism.

So, you can drink with your directs, as long as you generally do so equally across the entire team. Everyone doesn't have to be present every time you have a drink with your directs. You can have drinks with some team members one night and then be at a party with some others another night. As long as there is no appearance of favoritism, drinking with your directs is fine.

You Cannot Do or Say Stupid or Drunk Things with Your Directs

This, of course, is the obvious subtext of "drinking with one's directs."

It's not just the drinking with directs that's a problem; it's the stupid stuff that we say or do when we are drinking that's the problem. If we recommended against having drinks with directs, we'd have to tell you to shun one beer at the end of a day in the courtyard or one glass of wine at a going away dinner and ceremony.

These are the kinds of rules that get broken, and we miss the point of what the problem really is.

We know you're going to have opportunities to drink alcohol with your team. Not every dinner is an interview. Because you are the boss, you must drink responsibly. For most of us, two drinks puts us at or over the legal limit for drunk driving (and in some places it's less than one drink). If you get drunk with your direct friends, even though you don't have to drive and your directs are having a good time and "keeping up with you," they may have had too much. Are they going to ask you for a ride home? What will you do if they ask to come in to work late or to leave early in order to go to DUI classes because they got stopped? Do you doubt that everyone in the company will know that they were DUI after a party at which you were also over the limit but clearly not bothered by it?

Something else we've learned about drinking alcohol with directs: have only *one* drink with them. They'll appreciate your willingness to not set yourself apart from them completely. When you turn the second one down, they'll appreciate you more for setting an example and admitting you know you're *not* one of them, completely.

You Can "Friend" Your Directs on Facebook, but You Don't Have To

Because Facebook made a company and marketing decision to call the process of inviting someone into your personal network "friending," this entire discussion about friendship has become more complicated.

"Friending" someone on Facebook is NOT the same thing as being their friend. Being on someone's friend list on Facebook in no way causes there to be an assumption of friendship obligations.

Now, do you have to "friend" your directs on Facebook? No. Some of you may feel that if your boss asks, you have to say yes. You don't, but we've known plenty of bosses who are insecure enough to act as if their request carried with it their role power and a "no" wasn't even possible. (See? This stuff is messy!)

Most managers know that friending on Facebook isn't a given between managers and their directs. If everyone in your company does it, do not assume that the whole world does it also.

I know it's hard to hear that some friendships will have to become less important to you than your work responsibilities. We've felt that sting, and yet we've found over and over again that the best of friends totally respect it and understand it, and the relationship becomes better even as it becomes different. Effective managers want to know their directs, and they are required to make hard decisions that put the company first. Be a professional, and be friendly, not friends.

Can I Do One On Ones as a Project Manager?

You can have One On Ones in a matrix or matrix-hybrid organization as a project manager. You don't have to have line authority or control of directs who officially report to you to make it work. This type of One On One can work very well.

One reason is that matrix organizations reduce communication, and One On Ones directly improve communication. While we recommend One On Ones virtually exclusively for manager and team member relationships, the project manager and team member relationship has become important enough, and common enough, to justify this additional meeting.

The Key Difference Is a 15–15 Agenda versus a 10–10–10 Agenda

These are not pure One On Ones, because pure O3s occur between managers and their direct reports. Associates who are assigned to you on a project aren't true directs, so you won't have an O3 with them that is perfectly identical to a normal O3.

The big difference is that, rather than reserving 10 minutes of each half hour to (potentially) talk about the future, you eliminate those 10 minutes in favor of giving each participant 15 minutes to talk.

Why? Because these are NOT your directs, so you won't have much (if any) say in what their future will be. It's not to say that the future won't come up or that you won't have suggestions or insights to offer. Leave that to their manager.

Frankly, the best thing you can do to help their future is to help them be successful on your project. How do you do that? By focusing on Horstman's Law of Project Management: WHO does WHAT by WHEN. The way you can make one of your team members most effective on your project is by keeping that team member on track to meet their deliverables by the deadline.

So, the agenda for each Project Manager One On One (PMO3) is 15 minutes for the project team member, and 15 minutes for the project manager. They start with whatever they want to talk about, and they get 15 minutes to discuss whatever they want. After 15 minutes, you get 15 minutes to talk about what you need.

What should you do if the project team member wants to chat about the weekend despite pending deliverables that are in danger? That's fine. It's that person's 15 minutes. If that does happen, you simply take your 15 minutes and find out where the person is on each of his deliverables.

For most of the project managers who have learned about this concept, these PMO3s turn into miniature status updates. Team members tell us where they are, what issues they're facing, where they need help, and then we ask questions about what the status is and what their plans are to meet deliverable standards on time.

You might think that the weekly or biweekly project review does that, and you would be right. But we've been in hundreds of project review meetings ourselves, and the amount of professional, helpful candor that can appear in them, as opposed to blame shifting and defensiveness, is quite small. You can't give feedback. There are too many empty moments during which everyone knows what's going on but nobody wants to say it out loud. That's not a problem in PMO3s.

It also really helps to have a detailed project schedule and deliverables list each week. There is nothing wrong with using your 15 minutes to get a detailed status on everything a team member is responsible for in any way. "What is the status of X?" "What is the status of Y?" There are many things that would feel normal in a regular O3 held with a direct that are a lot less likely to come up in PMO3. Family and career are the two most common topics that are less likely to be brought up.

Follow the Basic Principles

Other than the 15–15 guidance, Project Manager O3s are nearly identical to standard O3s. Don't focus on the fact that the team member is "not a direct," so everything is up in the air. There's no sense in increasing the number of moving parts.

Focus on the Team Member

This is at the heart of ANY One On One. Because of the difference in role power—even in a project—between the project manager and the team member, to get good communication, you have to meet frequently and allow your project team member's agenda to come first. If you say, "It's about the project," you'll end up eroding the relationship, to the project's detriment at some point. If you say, "It's about the tasks," or "It's about the deadlines," you erode the relationship that comes from frequent communication about topics that are of value to the team member.

Even though it will feel more like a project update, the time dedicated to the team member and allowing the team member's agenda to take priority are core to the value of Project Manager O3s.

Scheduled, Weekly

The dedication of time holds the same important value to a project team member as it does to a direct. In some ways, it's especially reassuring, because the connection with you as project manager is more tenuous, so firm scheduling sends an even stronger message of commitment to the effort at communicating and building a relationship. Our general rule for the shortest project that benefits from PMO3s is three weeks. Most people probably think that's short and that we should have chosen a longer duration project. When we first started recommending these, we recommended six weeks, but so many project managers got value from the PMO3s that they kept lowering their lower limit and kept liking the value. Also, they generally found that at three weeks, projects seem short enough to be able to manage everything without PMO3s, but, in fact, three weeks is too long to keep everything in our heads or to rely on short deadlines or to ensure that deadlines are not missed and the project is delivered. Those project managers who do have PMO3s have told us that they start to RAISE that lower limit when they just have too many projects and they need to limit the number of meetings they have.

30 Minutes Long

An hour is too long: participants begin to dread them, and the PMO3s lose value. Less than 30 minutes doesn't feel like an investment is being made. Thirty minutes, in our experience, is the magic number, even for PMO3s

Your Cubicle or a Phone PMO3 Is Fine

Yes, you can have a PMO3 in your cubicle, usually. Some cubicles are too small, but that tends to be the exception rather than the rule. Phone PMO3s also are fine. We generally recommend that the project manager call the team member—that sends a message as well.

If (a big if) you feel that you can add this to a project launch meeting, introduce your plan for having PMO3s there. Walk your team members through the idea of PMO3s.

That being said, we know how project launches can be. Senior people who aren't delivering the project attend some of them. Project launch meetings are often much more about politics and image control, versus operational concerns. There are questions about who is running the launch (the sponsor or the project manager), agendas can be sketchy, and so forth. So, the launch may not be the time to introduce your plan for having PMO3s. You could certainly have another, team-member-only, meeting. But that's more likely to be a function of busyness and the culture of your organization.

One key difference between rolling out standard O3s and PMO3s is that you don't wait three weeks for everyone's schedule to clear. Early project successes—deadlines met, standards kept—are important bellwethers of overall success. Yes, people are busy. But work with your project team members to make those early meetings happen. Move things on your calendar to accommodate them, and then look three weeks into the future to see when would be a good time to have a standing meeting.

PMO3s Only Occur during the Life of the Project

When the project is over, the PMO3s stop. Resist any attempt by a team member to have them continue. The purpose no longer exists, their value decreases, and if the team member wants you to mentor her, that would be a different meeting purpose and periodicity.

You May Get More Pushback

Because you're not the team member's manager, you don't have the ability to use your role power to have the team member to participate. Further, the team member's manager CAN stop your efforts.

Team member pushback isn't uncommon, but it happens only about a third of the time, in our experience.

I recommend that you ask for the meeting first. Tell your team members the following:

1. This is how I manage projects.
2. It will help with communication.
3. It will last only 30 minutes once a week.
4. It will give you guaranteed time with me regularly, no matter what.

PMO3s will significantly reduce the bane of every project since the beginning of time: lack of communication.

6

How to Start Doing One On Ones

IF YOU'VE DECIDED TO START doing Manager Tools One On Ones, I'm excited for you. MTO3s will become the core of your managerial behavioral set.

Let's walk through, step-by-step, exactly what to do to get your O3s started.

Choose Times from Your Calendar

In order to send out an e-mail letting your team know that you're going to start doing One On Ones, you need to pick times on your calendar from which the team can choose their recurring appointment. Take the number of directs you have, multiply that number by 1.5, and that's the number of choices you need to make available to your team in your e-mail. If you have 10 directs, you need 15 half-hour time slots, or 7.5 hours.

Look at your calendar three to four weeks from now to choose the times. Don't look at this week or the next couple—you're probably too busy right now. Avoid times right before and after staff meetings, or regular meetings with your boss. Don't choose

Monday morning, because meetings slow people down, and you don't want to slow them down at the start of the week. Don't choose Friday afternoon, because if your O3 gets stepped on, you won't have time to reschedule. Some managers prefer to have all of their O3s on one day (if they don't have too many). Some managers prefer to spread them out. Our data are inconclusive about which works better—do what works for you.

Don't let your directs choose whatever time works for them. We've tested that. It will wreak havoc on your schedule. Each of your directs is only spending half an hour each week in O3s. You're spending—if you have 10 directs—*ten times* that amount. Your calendar is the one that needs protecting.

Don't choose times that work for you without any input. We've tested that. Directs won't like the times you choose for them, even if their calendar is as open as the Texas plains.

Don't lay out your calendar, and each of your direct's calendars, and try to figure out what will work best for you and each of them. We've tested that too—it also doesn't work.

The reason you need 15 half-hour slots if you have 10 directs is so the last direct who chooses still gets a choice. Don't worry—those five unused slots will come back to you.

Send Out a One-On-One E-mail Invitation

You can find a recommended text to use for the e-mail on our website link. Basically, it says that you're going to start doing weekly One On Ones in three to four weeks, it explains why you're doing them, and that your e-mail is to start the scheduling process. Give your directs 48 hours to respond with their chosen time. Tell them to "Reply to All" when they respond so that everyone will know which time slots have been taken. (Believe me, once the first time slot has been selected, your other directs will respond quickly.)

Allow for Possible Changes in the Near Future

The fact is, all great planners echo General Eisenhower's philosophy: planning is everything; plans are nothing. Things are going to change. Your boss is going to change the time for her weekly staff meeting. You're going to be put on a task force for some new project, somebody's child is going to make all-state band and have to be ferried to and fro. So, you set the schedule, and then after a few weeks, you allow for some changes, based on whether the schedule is working for both you and your directs.

Review Intent, Ground Rules, and O3 Agenda in Your Staff Meeting

Once you've sent the e-mail and set the schedule, set some time apart in your next staff meeting—say, 30 minutes—and walk everyone through what you've learned here. Walk them through the purpose, the agenda, how you're going to take notes, and how they're going to continue indefinitely. If you have questions about what might come up, please come to our website where we've got answers to all of them.

Answer Questions

Stand up in front of your directs and take questions from them. Don't be afraid of saying, "I don't know. We'll figure it out as we go. There's no way we can eliminate every hiccup with more planning. We'll get better at it as time goes by. We'll learn."

Conduct One On Ones Only for 12 Weeks

This is perhaps the most important concept in the rollout guidelines. You cannot effectively implement the entire "Management Trinity" all at once. It's too much to take in at one time. Your directs won't be able to absorb all of it. They won't like all that change. When there's too much change, none of it will proceed very well.

For 12 weeks, don't introduce any other new management behavioral change. Just work on One On Ones, for 12 weeks. At the end of the 12 weeks, you'll know your directs better, and you'll be much more aware of how to deliver the next steps.

Don't Rush to Get to Feedback!

If you start delivering feedback using our model after only a few weeks of O3s, you'll be learning two things at once. We've tested it, and it doesn't work. If you don't take time to build trust, your directs will struggle more and longer with getting more feedback from you.

Don't Rush to Get to Negative Feedback

Even if you are a nice person, there's a good chance that your directs have previously worked for a terrible manager. That terrible manager likely engaged in behaviors to hide her true intent. Your directs got smart and started waiting for the other shoe to drop. Don't do that to them by thinking you've mastered One On Ones and jumping too quickly into giving negative feedback. You'll deliver the negative feedback poorly, and you'll damage the trust you're trying to build in your MTO3s.

We'll cover why and how to deliver feedback—and how to roll it out—in the next two chapters.

7

Talk about
Performance—Feedback

THE SECOND CRITICAL MANAGER BEHAVIOR that leads to results and retention is communicating about performance.

To be fair, you probably tried to talk to your directs about how they were doing, but it was difficult, wasn't it? Particularly when you had to point out a mistake. You tried to talk to them about what had happened, but maybe they got upset, or you just didn't have the right words, and so the meeting was awkward. It chilled your relationship for a couple of weeks and was a performance dampener.

Don't despair. You were doing it wrong. So was I. And so were most other managers, for most of our careers. Feedback isn't inherently difficult to give, or to receive. (It's a great deal easier to give and receive feedback when trust has been built.) When you do it wrong, however, it feels *really* wrong to the direct. But doing it right just isn't all that difficult.

It probably doesn't feel great to read, "You were doing it wrong," but please let yourself off the hook. I did it wrong, too, for years, and sometimes I still do. Most of my clients, colleagues, and friends who are effective managers all did it wrong for years, until they learned better. Yes, communicating about your directs' performance is part of your job, and yes, it's unlikely you've been doing it at a very high level, but you can be forgiven for not having done it much or done it well. Why? Because you've never been taught how.

In fact, I'd bet part of the reason you're reading this book is that you were given virtually no training as a manager when you first ascended to the role. You may have wanted to do the job. You may have had a sense that, based on what *you* wanted from *your* boss, you would be able to give that kind of guidance and support if you were a boss. It probably hasn't worked out that way.

This makes you completely normal. If, when you observe other managers, they look like they get it, you're likely mistaken. They're as untrained as you are, for the most part. If they seem confident of their managerial skills, they're probably not. They hope, much like you do, that their lack of skills and knowledge won't be discovered.

The average manager hasn't been trained, tutored, mentored, taught, or coached with anything approaching professional development of the skills necessary for becoming a successful manager.

This lack of skills and training shows up most quickly in your lack of ability to communicate about performance. You know you're supposed to, and you've tried, but it hasn't gone well, has it?

I suspect the following happened to you early on as a manager. You noticed that one of your directs had done poorly, or less than well, at something. You resolved to say something to the direct. You thought about it a bit, and you had a couple of bullet points in your mind that you were going to mention to the direct. You knew this was part of your job, and you knew you didn't know *exactly* what you were doing. But you also trusted that your direct probably knew that he had made a mistake and expected you to say something. Also, you had a good relationship with your direct, so you thought the meeting would go okay.

Because you had heard the phrase, "Praise in public, criticize in private," you brought the direct into your office. You made small talk for 30 to 60 seconds, thinking that's what you would do before a normal conversation. This made sense to you, because you wanted this conversation to be normal.

You said what you had planned to say, mostly. You didn't say it exactly right, because all you had was a couple of bullet points. You decided to say a little more, to sort of, in your mind, "soften the blow." It was all so clear in your plan, so clear in your mind.

But it went poorly, didn't it? The direct pushed back and maybe even interrupted. She told you why she did what she did (which sounded perfectly reasonable). She became visibly frustrated, waited until you ran out of words, and asked, "Is that all?" and then left.

So, maybe the next time you decided that you'd give the feedback indirectly. One of your directs had shown up late to meetings a couple of times and didn't seem to care very much, but you weren't going to give him the chance to push back or give you his reasons. Frankly, there was a part of you that didn't care about his reasons. Asking him to be on time wasn't too much to ask.

So, the next time this direct came late to a meeting, you waited until the meeting broke up, and you shared a final comment with everyone: "Look, guys, I need you to get to meetings on time, okay? That's not too much to ask." You weren't being confrontational or pointing the finger at any one person; you were simply and clearly stating the standard of behavior you expected.

That feedback didn't work *either*. The direct to whom you were indirectly sending the feedback didn't change his behavior, and your best performer, who was always on time, seemed irritated, and perhaps rightly so, since he was always on time.

All of these errors are normal, everyday occurrences in organizations all over the world. You're not alone.

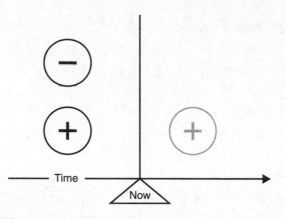

Figure 7.1 The Basics of Feedback

Before we learn the details of the Manager Tools Feedback Model, let's first change your perception about what the purpose of feedback is. If you know the purpose, it's much easier to get your delivery right or to correct it when you get off track.

Consider the simple illustration of the basics of feedback, shown in Figure 7.1.

Assume that you are at the "Now" moment in Figure 7.1. It's noon, on a workday. Time flows from left to right. What happened this morning is represented on the left of the figure, and the future—this afternoon and beyond—is represented on the right.

This morning, one of your directs engaged in some behavior, either good or bad. The plus inside the circle represents the direct's good behavior, and the minus inside the circle represents a mistake she made.

It's now noon, and you have become aware of her mistake: you read a report, you received an e-mail from her, you watched her give a presentation, or a colleague shared something about her with you. Now you have to decide what to do. Of course, the classic response is to do nothing.

The direct probably knows she messed up; she'll self-correct. If it's something good, there's no need to say anything, since she was just doing her job. You can't go around praising people doing their jobs, or they'll get addicted to the praise.

However, you want more input from *your* boss about how *you're* doing, so you vow, here and now, to say something. Great. You think to yourself, "Okay, what do I say to her about what she did?" *And this is where it all goes wrong.*

When the average manager gives feedback, *the focus is on what happened.* The manager thinks about what happened in the past and asks herself how to talk to the direct—about what happened, in the past, about which the manager can do nothing.

It ought to be obvious why talking about something that happened in the past is a problem. It also ought to give you a clue as to why directs get defensive when managers talk to them about their mistakes. *They get defensive because managers talk to them about their mistakes—which happened in the past—about which the directs can do nothing.* So, they feel trapped.

Have you ever noticed that your directs often respond to your corrective comments with all the reasons *why* they did whatever it was they did? You can probably work out why by asking yourself two questions:

1. *Have I made any mistakes in the last month?* If you're like the rest of us, you'll privately admit, "yes, a number of them, if I'm being honest."
2. *Did I intend to make those mistakes? Did I set out to mess things up on purpose?* If you're like the rest of us, you'll immediately say, and perhaps vehemently, "No, of course I didn't."

Well, remember, our directs are similar to us. They made mistakes, but they weren't actively trying to mess things up. *They had good reasons for the mistakes they made!* So, of course they're going to respond to a discussion about their mistake by giving their reasons for doing what they did. The mistake may not be good, but at least their reasons were.

There are all kinds of reasons why directs defend themselves. Probably first on the list is a lack of trust in you, their boss. The solution to this we already talked about earlier in this book: frequent, high-quality communication between you and them, through Manager Tools One On Ones.

The lack of frequent performance communications increases directs' defensiveness as well. If performance communications are rare, then every one of them takes on increased significance. If you don't point out mistakes frequently, your directs assume that, when you do choose to talk to them, they think it's because they *may* be "in trouble." Their defensiveness, then, should not be surprising.

Also, let's face it: our role power increases their defensiveness. We control their addiction to food, clothing, and shelter, remember? Challenge someone who fears you at some level, and you'll get some pushback.

The way to reduce these problems down to a manageable minimum is to ask yourself, "What is the purpose of this performance communication that I'm delivering? *The purpose of performance communications (and therefore feedback) is to* **encourage effective future behavior.**

Encourage Effective Future Behavior

Each of those four words is important, but perhaps the most important one is *future*. If you talk to your directs with the intent of pointing out their mistakes (or even their successes), you doom the conversation to being about the past, about which you or they can do nothing. The moment you switch to a future focus, however, you free yourself up to *focus on something that you (and they) can do something about.*

Look again at Figure 7.1. You'll note that in the past (this morning) there are two circles: one positive and one negative. In the future, there is only one circle, a positive one. Can you see why that is? The positive circle is there because that's all you want in the future: effective behavior.

Rather than thinking, "What can I say to this person about her mistake?" or, "How can I praise her for that great decision?" the right approach is to focus on what you want (the future), not on the past, because there's nothing she or you can do about the past.

Regardless of whether your direct was ineffective or effective this morning, the true purpose of any performance communication about either situation is exactly the same: you want more effective behavior in the future. If your direct made a mistake, you want different behavior. If your direct did something well, you want more of the same.

When you realize this, you realize you're not very interested in the mistake itself when it comes to talking about performance. Sure, you want to know what the mistake was, but you can't do anything about it, because it's already happened. The only question is, can you encourage the direct not to do it again?

Focus on what you want, and don't worry about exactly how you're going to word some criticism or about how to praise someone.

The best way to encourage effective future behavior is the Manager Tools Feedback Model. It's very different probably from what you're used to, because your fundamental premise about feedback—talking about what happened—is wrong.

The Manager Tools Feedback Model has four simple steps:

Step 1: Ask.

Step 2: State the Behavior.

Step 3: State the Impact of the Behavior.

Step 4: Encourage Effective Future Behavior.

Step 1: Ask

The first step of the Manager Tools Feedback Model is simple: ask your direct if you can give the direct some feedback. You can use the word *feedback* or another word, but you must first ask the direct, every time, whether it's positive feedback that you will be giving or negative feedback. The question might be something like this:

"Can I give you some feedback?"

"Can I make an observation?"

"Can I share something with you?"

"Can I have a word with you?"

The reason you should ask for permission is that the only person who can engage in the behavior is the team member to whom you're talking. Of course, you know that you can't "make" them do anything. They have to want to do it themselves.

There is no point in talking to a member of your team about *his own future behaviors* if he has just come into the building after having a difficult conversation with a colleague, or he's just come out of a difficult meeting, or he has to finish creating a spreadsheet against a deadline. The direct needs to be able to listen and hear you in order for you to be sure that the direct will be at least able to understand what future behaviors you want him to engage in.

Asking (and honoring a "no" response, if it is given) enables you to make sure that the direct is listening. To make this clear, before we ever use the Manager Tools Feedback Model with our team, we brief them about it first. (We will explain how to do this in the next chapter.) They'll know that, because we told them that when we ask, they CAN say no.

It's an important managerial rule to never ask a question of your directs if you don't intend to honor their answer. If you asked to give them feedback, and are told no and then simply go ahead, you would prove that you don't care about their answers. That would cause them in the future to realize they don't need to give you an honest answer. Going forward they'll simply start telling you what they think you want to hear.

Relatedly, it's possible that a direct may say no repeatedly to avoid getting feedback. It's exceedingly rare, but that being said, There's a Cast for That™.

We have found that, in more than three-fourths of situations (self-reported by managers), in which directs say no to the question, they seek the manager out within a few hours to find out what the feedback would have been. I've been told by many directs that their curiosity got the better of them. What better way to give feedback to a direct than when they come ask for it?

Now, if you're like a lot of managers, asking bothers you a little. You think to yourself, "Wait, I'm the boss, so why should I have to ask?" There are several reasons you should ask first, but there is only one that really matters: *Asking directs for permission to give them feedback significantly increases their appreciation for your giving them the feedback and also the likelihood of their effective future behavior.*

It really boils down to this: *do you want to be the boss, or do you want your team to be more effective?* (Assume you can't have both.)

We don't ask only when we're going to give negative feedback. We ask every time. If we only asked when we were going to give negative feedback, our directs would soon understand that this was a signal and would know what was coming next. For this reason, we also ask the same question every time.

Before we walk through the rest of the Manager Tools Feedback Model, you'll notice that the model starts out scripted. It stays that way, on purpose. For years, managers have told us: "I don't know what to say." So, we created the model to eliminate that stumbling block. Manager Tools has tried to make it very simple to give feedback, in order to encourage more managers to give more feedback. We want you to memorize the words in the model, so all you have to think about is the behavior of the direct.

Being a little bit scripted and maybe even awkward—for a short time—in the service of giving your directs what you know they want is a reasonable price to pay for more effectiveness.

At some point, you'll be so comfortable with the model and its subtleties that you'll be able to not use the phrasings so precisely and still get across to your directs what you need to. Eventually, they'll know the structure and be able to understand you clearly.

Using this method is easier than sitting around, knowing you should say something, and thinking, "I don't know what to say."

Step 2: State the Behavior

In step 2, we tell the direct what she did well or what she did that we would like her to change. We say, "When you (insert behavior) . . ."

We use the word "behavior" *very precisely*.

What Is Behavior? Behavior consists of five things, as we define it.

- **The Words You Say.** There's a difference, audible and measurable, between the sales rep who asks, "Can I place that order?" and the one who says, "I hope you'll consider placing an order." Both may mean well (both surely would say they meant well), but meaning well and saying those two things will likely get them different results in the long run.

  The words you choose to say out loud to others are a choice, and different words produce different results. *Your choice of words makes a difference in business results.* Furthermore, certain words are known to produce distinctly better results in certain situations.

  If you asked a direct to lead a project, and she said, "That would be great," you'd probably see that as a positive attitude about her effort. If, however, she said, "okay," you might wonder how committed she was. Both responses are positive, but the words are different and they would probably mean differing levels of enthusiasm to you.

On a lighter note, suppose the love of your life said, in passing, as you both were waiting in line in front of a theater concessions stand, "I'd like to marry you. Do you want popcorn?" We suspect that those are not the words you'd prefer to hear, and, what's more, *you would argue that there are more effective words, and the words affect the meaning of the statement significantly*.

Even if the intent is the same, the words matter if they're likely to influence the outcome.

■ **How You Say Those Words.** The tone and tenor of your words and the speed and inflection with which you say them can change your meaning—intentionally or not—enormously.

Our friend, Michael Swenson, uses the string of words, "I didn't say you had an attitude problem," to illustrate this beautifully.

If you say, "**I** didn't say you had an attitude problem," well, then, someone else did, but you still have an attitude problem, most likely.

If you say, "I didn't *say* you had an attitude problem," well, then, I surely implied it to allow your inference.

If you say, "I didn't say you had an *attitude* problem," well, then, I must mean that you've surely got some other kind of problem. The actual words are the same, but *how you say them* makes an enormous difference in others' perception of your meaning.

■ **Your Facial Expressions.** Usually, smiling when you agree to do something extra for a customer is perceived by customers as being more professional than furrowing your brow and not smiling at all.

You might say that you mean nothing by your facial expression but communication is what the listener does. You're still responsible for what you say, but you can't control how your listener interprets it. Meaning is determined 7 percent based on the words we use, 38 percent by tonal differences, and 55 percent by nonverbal cues (facial expressions and body language).

When you hear someone express an idea that someone else is excited about and you choose not to smile, as an example, you are allowing them to infer that you are NOT excited about the idea. If you've only just heard it, that's seen as a quick disregarding of someone else's hard work. Perhaps you're right, but don't be surprised by the other person's inference.

■ **Body Language.** Crossing one's arms isn't always just a response to the cold. Looking down when you are asked a direct question isn't perceived the same way as giving a response with eye contact. Drumming your fingers on a conference room table may "mean nothing," but most people would argue that point with you.

Suppose a direct, when asked about her status on a project said, "Pretty good," while smiling, nodding her head, and looking directly into your eyes. Another of your directs said, "Pretty good," after pausing, looking down, and then looking away. Can you honestly say that both answers meant the exact same thing to you?

This is not to say that one direct is right and the other is wrong. But there is general agreement about the differences, and what they mean in terms of effectiveness toward achieving results.

■ **Work Product.** What you do and how well you do your job are behaviors as well. As a general rule, work product behavior is defined more specifically as:

  ○ *Quality*: How does your work compare to accepted standards of effectiveness and excellence?

- ○ *Quantity*: How much work have you done? This is certainly true in many jobs where there are numerical goals. There are also many jobs that are not formally measured where quantity and efficiency can be assessed.
- ○ *Accuracy*: Does your work require rework, or does it meet generally accepted practices in your profession?
- ○ *Timeliness*: Do you meet deadlines? Speed can sometimes create inefficiencies, but usually it is an enormous competitive advantage. Frequency of work product is also a part of timeliness. One's own timeliness is included, too—being where you're supposed to be when you're supposed to be there.
- ○ *Documents*: You're responsible for the communication (and analysis and ideas) you present to others in written and electronic form. E-mails are behavior: you made choices about what you said and how you said it. This is very much akin to the words you say and how you say them, as mentioned earlier.

You'll notice that neither attitude nor motivation are parts of behavior. Far too many of us managers think that our job is to see/ hear/read the behavior; infer the underlying intent/motivation/ attitude that drives it; and address the underlying intent/attitude. But that doesn't work, for two reasons: we're bad at guessing what others' intent is, and our directs know they can argue about what's in their head, because we can't prove that was "actually" their intent.

Of course it's true that attitudes and motivations drive behaviors, but they're not visible, and we can only guess at them. Therefore, we don't give feedback on what directs meant, or why they did something, or what their attitude was when they did something.

Consider this scenario: A manager is in a meeting with her direct, who interrupts, rolls his eyes, and crosses his arms when others share ideas. It's obvious he "has a bad attitude," and later the manager calls him on it.

Manager: You had a bad attitude in that meeting.
Direct: No I didn't!

Giving feedback on attitude—because it's not behavior, and not visible—leads to defensive behavior on the part of the direct; at this point, he is not listening or considering how he can change his behavior. The direct knows that the manager cannot "know" his attitude or mental state at all, so he can argue it without losing.

Contrast the manager's previous comment with the following one:

Manager: When you roll your eyes, interrupt, and cross your arms . . .

Step 2 of the model always begins with the words, *When you*. By starting your sentence with these words, you encourage yourself to focus on the direct's behavior.

Here are some examples:

"When you are ahead of schedule . . ."
"When you stay an extra hour to find the root cause . . ."
"When you respond politely after the customer insults you . . ."
"When you make that extra call to keep the customer informed . . ."
"When you promise it to me yesterday but don't deliver . . ."

When you are personally my two favorite words in the Manager Tools Feedback Model. I find that when I start step 2 with "when you" it makes it easier to focus on their behavior and the impact, and for me to be simple, casual, and quick. It forces me to stay away from telling a story or giving some background.

Directs don't want managers to sugarcoat negative feedback. They don't want them to work their way toward saying something. They don't want chit-chat. More words *do not soften the blow*. They just want managers to say what needs to be said.

Would you rather have a 15-second negative feedback discussion or a two-minute negative feedback discussion with your boss? Shorter is better. Saying "When you" will help you be brief.

Step 3: State the Impact of the Behavior

In step 3, we state the impact that the direct's behavior has had. These words form the effect part of cause and effect, the reaction part of action and reaction, and the response part of incident and response. Unless you do step 3, the direct will not necessarily understand the problem or the positive impact their behavior has had on the organization, the team, and those around them.

Here is a simple example. You and your boss sit very close together. One of your directs has a habit of reporting bad news to you in person. If you're not at your desk, he assumes that you would want him to inform your boss, because it saves you a step and your boss is going to find out anyway. (Don't laugh, this actually happened). Of course, what happens is that your boss now knows before you do, and when he attacks you for the bad news, you don't know what he's talking about. Your direct doesn't know that happens and that it ruins your day. And, why would he: he had a legitimate reason for sharing with your boss.

In this instance, the negative feedback might be:

Manager: Can I give you some feedback?
Direct: Sure, boss.

Manager: When you tell my boss bad news before me, even with the best of intentions, I end up getting in a lot of trouble for not knowing before he did. Can you try to tell me first, going forward?

Here's a positive example: Your direct stayed late last night to help a new hire get oriented. He showed the new hire what the copier code was, how to fill out expense reports, and so on. This morning the new hire came by to pass along thanks for your direct staying late. Giving feedback to your experienced direct might sound like this:

Manager: Can I give you some feedback?
Direct: Of course, boss, what's up?
Manager: When you stayed late last night, and showed the new guy how to fill out expense reports, well, that's a classy thing to do. And, the new guy came by my desk to offer thanks—it meant a lot to him. Thanks.

You might be thinking at this point, "wait, this isn't 'feedback.' My boss doesn't ever talk to me about small things like this. If I ever get negative performance communications, it's a big deal, there's a pattern, and I feel like I'm getting in trouble. These examples don't sound like that."

You're partially right. While what we're discussing actually is feedback, your experience has been more akin to punishment than feedback. What you've experienced is what most managers do for performance warranting some negative performance communications: wait and wait and wait until they finally "have" to have a "conversation" about an "issue." And it's usually at the end of the day, and both of you leave the conversation feeling awful.

But effective feedback isn't about waiting until there's a pattern, and it doesn't get better with age. And wouldn't you rather know sooner rather than later that there's a problem? Wouldn't you rather your boss talk to you before there's a "pattern" that means you're "in trouble"? Wouldn't you rather be talked to when the problem is small and you can make a small correction, an easy correction, rather than creating a habit that's hard to break because nobody told you earlier that what you were doing wasn't working?

Our guidance is to look for small impacts that happen every day. It's easier to give feedback on them, and all those small changes will add up.

Beginning step 3 with "Here's what happens" will help you remember the Manager Tools Feedback Model and formulate the feedback properly. Once you're confident, you can leave out those three words.

Here are some examples of this step:

> *"I can focus on other areas that need my attention."*
>
> *"Here's what happens: the customer calls to thank me."*
>
> *"Here's what happens: I notice your extra effort."*
>
> *"I appreciate it, and the team's job is much easier."*
>
> *"Our case for the new hire is that much stronger."*
>
> *"The project stays green, and we dodge a political bullet."*

Did you notice that these were all positive?

Step 4: Encourage Effective Future Behavior

In step 4, we either ask for a change in behavior or say thank you for behavior that we want to encourage.

With affirming/positive feedback, the direct now has a specific understanding of the behavior that was effective and the impact that it has. This is the power of giving feedback using this model rather than making a praise-like statement of "good job." You have a method that encourages long-term effective behavior.

Two examples of Step 4 when it's positive are, "Thanks" and "Please keep it up."

When we are giving negative feedback, we are asking the direct to behave differently. We're not punishing the past mistake, because we've already forgiven it. Remember that our focus is on the future, not the past.

The easiest way to ask the direct to do this is, "Can you change that?" All this requires from the direct is an affirmative answer. Once you and your directs are comfortable with the model, you can also use "What can you do differently?" This is a more difficult question, because it requires the direct to come up with an alternative right away.

Here are some examples:

"Could you change that?"

"Can you do that differently?"

"What can you do differently?"

"How could that be better?"

Here are several examples of putting it all together.

Manager: "Can I give you some feedback?"
Direct: "Sure."
Manager: "When you're ahead of schedule on Project X, I can focus on other areas that need my attention. Thanks."

■ ■ ■

Manager: "Can I make an observation?"
Direct: "Of course."
Manager: "When you respond politely after the customer insults you, the customer calls to thank me. Well done."

Manager: "Can I share something with you?"

Direct: "Yes."

Manager: "When you promise to give me the data yesterday but miss that deadline, I have to scramble to put everything together. Can you work on that, please?"

If you'll practice, you can deliver feedback in 5 to 15 seconds. At our Effective Manager conferences, we give feedback to five to six people in a row, and our presenters can do it in 40 to 45 seconds. It's quick, it's easy, and the directs warm to it quickly.

Again, the four steps:

Step 1: Ask.

Step 2: State the Behavior.

Step 3: State the Impact of the Behavior.

Step 4: Encourage Effective Future Behavior.

When Should I Give Feedback?

Giving immediate feedback is ideal. When athletes perform, they take an action, and they get an immediate response to their action. They can adjust based on what happens. When we drive, we turn the wheel, and the car responds. When we say something in a conversation, the person we're talking to responds quickly.

Imagine these same things happening but with delayed feedback. What if there was a 30-second delay for the car to respond when we turned the wheel? What if we had to wait 30 minutes for someone to respond to our conversation? What if we had to wait 30 days to hear about how something we did at work didn't work out the way we wanted it to? When you really start thinking about it, we take feedback for granted in virtually every aspect of our lives. We also take for granted that we're going to get it fairly quickly. But for some reason we don't seem to get that from our manager.

Whenever possible, it's best for managers to give feedback immediately after they see, hear, or notice the behavior. If you have a chance to give feedback right after one of your directs does something you either want to encourage (positive feedback) or change (negative feedback), and you can do so without others overhearing, do so. If you're in a One On One, and the direct you're with disparages someone inappropriately, give the direct negative feedback right then. If you're in a meeting, and one of your team suggests a great idea, lean over and whisper some positive feedback if you can do so privately. If you're walking out of a meeting, and your direct just solved a problem, tell him so privately with some positive feedback while you walk together back to your cubicle. If you get a note from a peer manager with some kind words for one of your team, walk over to her cubicle, and quietly provide some positive feedback.

The point of immediacy is not to wait. The sooner your directs get feedback about what they do, good or bad, the more quickly they can implement that feedback. If managers can give feedback immediately, it works better.

But "immediately" isn't *necessary*. If you can't give someone feedback in a meeting because you can't do it without others overhearing, you can absolutely give it an hour or two later, when you and they have a moment. Another way to think about the "when" of feedback is "as soon as is practicable"—but that's not as easy to say as "immediately."

Even though it's great to be able to give immediate feedback, truly "immediate" feedback is highly unlikely. Too often, there are others around; you don't find out about the behavior until a day or two later; or you may tell yourself that you don't have time to walk over and take 30 seconds to deliver the feedback.

In fact, being able to give immediate feedback is so unlikely that we at Manager Tools have learned that questions about feedback are often a red herring. We've learned that, when managers ask about giving immediate feedback, it's a setup. They're not really asking about when to give feedback. They want to hear us say that "Immediate is best" so that they can then describe why that means they *can't* actually give immediate feedback because *immediate* isn't possible because of all the examples we just described.

Frankly, most managers know that immediate feedback is really hard to achieve. And so they make the perfection—which is immediate feedback—the enemy of the good—which is *feedback as soon as is practicable*.

Immediate is a strong word. It means "at once," or "in that instant." Some managers seem to think that, if one of our team says something great in a meeting, giving that person feedback after the meeting is NOT effective because it wasn't immediate. They say, "Well, immediate is virtually impossible, and waiting to the end of a meeting isn't immediate, so I can't do that."

It's really impressive to discover the logical knots some managers will tie themselves in to avoid having a pleasant 10-second conversation with one of their directs—a conversation that the direct has asked for and that they themselves want from their own bosses; that *every* direct says that he or she wants, even if it's given in a clumsy manner.

When you *can* give immediate feedback, do so, and relish the moment. Your direct will, too. Give yourself credit for the equivalent of *two* feedback moments when your feedback is immediate.

Just remember that truly immediate feedback isn't the standard. If you can't give feedback immediately, this doesn't mean that you can't give it; it just means it won't be immediate.

The Simple Answer Is, Sooner Is Better

Giving immediate feedback is a great but almost unattainable goal. The real goal for timing your feedback is as soon as you can. When you learn about something positive or negative that one of your directs does, decide to share it with the direct as feedback when you next have 30 seconds with the direct. Usually, that will be very quickly—within a day or two for most managers.

A day or two later, for most directs and most managers, in most situations, is a completely reasonable, appropriate, and effective timeline for giving feedback, whether the feedback is positive or negative. If you give feedback within an hour, that's great. The value of feedback doesn't decline appreciably within the first three to five days the vast majority of the time.

If you keep in mind that sooner is better and that there's no appreciable decline in value during the first three to five days, you have a lot more time and a lot more opportunities to deliver what it is your directs want—and tell us they want.

If you're wondering how to define *how long "soon" lasts at the outside, it's about a week.* In other words, don't give feedback that's more than a week old. Why? The reason is that your ability to remember precisely by then has faded enough so that you may not get it right, and accuracy matters when you are giving feedback. You shouldn't say something vague like, "I can't remember what you said, but whatever it was, it was really good and made us look good." That's not really feedback. A delay of more than a week in giving feedback will seem to the direct as having to do with hesitancy on your part or doubts about the direct. A long delay is perceived by directs whom we've asked as reflecting on the quality of the feedback you're delivering.

Further, your direct won't remember the moment as clearly as you would have liked him to. Even if your recollection is precise, the direct's recollection may not be. We see an increase in comments or questions along the lines of, "Is that what happened, really?" or, "I don't remember it that way." Such responses are antithetical to encouraging effective behavior in the future. You'll get more of this when you give negative rather than positive feedback, obviously.

So, the absolute longest we recommend you could delay in giving feedback is about a week after you have learned of the behavior. The problem, though, is that we all seem to define *a week* differently, and some of us can't really keep track of when a week ago was. Today is Friday of this week, the behavior I saw happened Monday of last week, and that's "a week ago." Also, we've had managers say, "Well, it happened, I think, on Tuesday, but maybe it was Wednesday. It's now Wednesday, a week later. Should I give feedback?"

We've discovered a sharper dividing line. If what you noticed or heard about happened *before your last One On One*, as a general rule, don't give feedback about it. This is Manager Tools' recommended way to measure how long a week ago has been.

Yes, if you had your One On One yesterday, this guideline suggests that something that happened two days ago is too long ago to give feedback on. Maybe that's stretching our guideline a little bit further than we intend. But, don't be worried that you won't be able to give feedback about what you saw two days ago, because you can expect to see more of the same behavior coming up again fairly soon.

8

Common Questions and Resistance to Feedback

How Does It Sound?

Positive and negative feedback sound identical. If this statement surprises you, go back and look at the feedback graphic in Figure 7.1. Our purpose sits on the right, and it's a positive future. That purpose is the same whether it's positive or negative feedback.

Mike once told me, "I only give (negative) feedback when I can chuckle about it." That's a perfect attitude. He knows that if he can't chuckle about it, there's a chance he's going to deliver it with some negativity, perhaps even with some judgment or mild anger. He's learned that, while it may feel good to vent, in the long run, it's ineffective. This is a lesson I am personally still learning also. I still catch myself wanting to give negative feedback because I'm angry about a mistake. The anger is what's driving my desire, *not my direct's effective future behavior*. So I wait, like Mike.

Mike's approach reminds me of a manager who was really struggling with the Manager Tools Feedback Model. He had had incredible success with One On Ones. He was surprised to hear what

127

his directs shared with him in the MTO3s. He was getting to know what made them tick much better. He was also stunned that, even though he was worried about the time the O3s would take out of his calendar, he seemed to have even more free time than he thought.

However, what came next was disappointing. The manager told us how he was *really* struggling with giving feedback. He said, "They all recoil in fear *every time*. Morale has *plummeted*, even though it had gone up because of the MTO3s. Now, even One On Ones have gone downhill, too. It's a disaster."

I asked, "Why don't you walk me through what you're doing when you give feedback?" It's been my experience coaching managers that giving feedback in theory is almost always different from giving feedback in practice. Here is the type of feedback this manager would give his directs.

Manager: "Mark, can I give you some feedback?"

Direct: "Yep."

Manager: "When you behave like THAT, let me tell you something. You make me angry QUICK. I think to myself, 'If THAT happens a couple of times, you're a big problem for me, a problem I'm not happy about.' What are you gonna do about this?"

His demeanor was *very* direct (and I'm being kind). I felt like there was meanness, power, and intimidation in his delivery.

This was not feedback delivered well. Sure, he asked; sure, he used the word *feedback*, he said "When you," and he ended with a question about the future. But it's still not Manager Tools feedback, because it violates the purpose of the feedback: to encourage effective future behavior. He wasn't encouraging anything. He was threatening retribution through his role power. I helped him understand how his approach was completely off, and recommended he apologize for his mistakes, and start with feedback again. He did, and things improved. Slowly.

The following are some questions to ask yourself as you think about delivering feedback to your directs.

Question 1: Am I Angry?

If you're angry, *don't give feedback*. Period.

If your directs sense that you're angry, they are *not* going to be receptive, even if they *say* they are by answering yes to step 1. Further, even if they *are* in a receptive mind-set, you are not in a delivering mind-set. Your directs are not going to be *encouraged* if they think you're *angry*. And, look, you're not Brad Pitt. You're not Meryl Streep. If you're angry, you can't act your way out of it. You can't fool your team. They know when you're angry.

If you're struggling with delivering feedback—because you've been getting a less than great response from your directs—and you're a high-energy person, or a perfectionist who gets angry about little things, this is an important question to ask yourself before you give feedback.

If your directs know you're angry, then the feedback is about you and not about them, and that violates the purpose of the feedback, both in terms of encouraging good behavior and in terms of changing bad behavior. Even more simply, it won't work.

Question 2: Do I Want to Remind or Punish?

If your purpose is to remind your directs of their mistakes, again, that is not in alignment with the purpose of giving feedback. If you're giving feedback, then your purpose is to encourage effective future behavior. Yes, you have to mention the past, but that's not your purpose. You're not trying to point out the mistake.

Question 3: Can I Let It Go?

If you can't let it go in terms of how you feel, we recommend that you *do* let it go by not giving the negative feedback. We've found over and over again that managers who feel an urge to deliver feedback are doing it for the wrong reasons. We don't want to confuse the need for delivering feedback quickly with an emotional *urge* to do so. The manager who really believes in the purpose of feedback and wants to focus on encouraging effective future behavior isn't in a negative emotional rush to give feedback.

If you can't pause, you may have too much energy at that time to deliver feedback that will encourage effective behavior in the future.

Maybe Delay or Defer

What should you do if you don't pass the three-question checklist?

First, if you *do* pass the three-question checklist, go ahead and deliver the feedback. If you're not angry, if it's not about the past or about punishment, and if you can let it go, then go ahead and give the feedback.

If you don't pass the three-question checklist, what should you do? You should either delay or defer. *Delay* means you hold off giving feedback for a bit. Maybe you will get over being angry. Maybe you will realize that, in your haste, your thinking was sloppy. Then you would be back on track, moving toward where your purpose is to encourage effective future behavior. You realize that you can let it go, so it's okay to have that 15-second feedback conversation, after a delay of a few hours, or overnight.

Delay is okay. It's only one piece of feedback, and a few hours won't hurt.

Suppose you pause and realize a few hours later that you're still not in the right place. You're still angry, or, for any other reason, you're just not where you should be. That's fine. Defer the feedback completely. Let this instance go completely. Don't give the negative feedback about the behavior.

It's okay. Remember that feedback is about the future, right? Suppose you don't give the negative feedback, and then, for whatever reason, the behaviors that you were going to address don't occur again. Seriously, what's wrong with that? Just take credit for the magical change! Doing nothing worked.

And what if it doesn't work? What if the behavior comes back? Then it's simply time for more feedback. Just answer the checklist questions again before you deliver the feedback.

What Do I Do If One of My Directs Pushes Back or Refuses Feedback?

We think many newer managers are stunned into a kind of muteness when their direct pushes back or refuses feedback. The answer is *The Shot across the Bow*.

The Shot across the Bow concept of handling defensive responses to feedback is based on the naval concept of shooting across the bow of an opposing vessel. When a Navy or a Coast Guard ship wants to warn someone, they fire a "shot across their bow." They don't fire a warning shot, per se. A shot across the bow is a specific thing.

There are two things that make the shot across the bow distinctive. First, in order to shoot across the enemy's bow, the enemy ship must be within range. The shot across their bow shows them that they can be reached. Second, because the aiming point is a specific place—forward of amidships, behind the prow—when you shoot there, you prove that you can hit what you are aiming at. Basically, a shot across the bow says, "I can reach you, and I can hit you if I want to."

The analogy works this way: when your direct gets defensive, *you needn't do anything at all about it, because you have already fired a shot across their bow.* They likely know they're in the wrong, and they know you're aware of what they did. If it continues, you'll likely be back. Enough said.

And let's go back to the purpose of feedback: encouraging effective *future* behavior. If your direct becomes defensive, he is being defensive about what happened, or why it happened, or that it didn't happen. These are all arguments *about the past.*

You initiated the conversation, and your purpose was a request about the future. Your direct wants to argue about the past. Why should you give up your purpose—the future—in order to go back into the past when we both know there's *no way* you're going to win that argument about the past with a defensive direct? And, even if you did, is there any chance that you could then figuratively drag the direct back to your original purpose and have her agree with you about what you want in the future? Of course not.

So, if your stuck-in-the-past direct won't allow you to achieve your original purpose, don't honor the direct's request that you join her in the past. It was your conversation to begin with. If you're not going to be able to achieve your purpose, don't make it worse by arguing about something you can't change.

In other words, *we recommend that you give in when a direct argues or gets defensive.* Don't get drawn into a discussion about who said what, what she meant, what you saw, what she actually did, who reported the behavior to you, how she has different priorities, how you don't have her technical skills, or how she was trying something new. Do not discuss with the direct what happened. None of these topics is about the future you want to focus on.

Once you've given the feedback and the direct has pushed back, pause, smile, apologize, and walk away. You've made your point. Don't let the direct try to win her argument simply because you've shown her the courtesy of letting go.

The conversation might sound like this:

Manager: Can I give you some feedback?

Direct: Sure, what is it?

Manager: When you're late to a staff meeting, we have to rearrange the agenda. Can you change that going forward? . . .

Direct: Geez! Is that all you ever see—mistakes and lateness? Traffic was horrible! My e-mail wasn't downloading! Give me a break!

Manager: (backing away, smiling) You know what, let's forget it. Bad timing, you're forgiven. No worries.

Remember again what this all boils down to: *does the direct change her behavior in the future?* She's much more likely to do so if you avoid the arguments she's trying to put in the path of an effective conversation.

The Capstone: Systemic Feedback

What do you do when you've tried giving negative feedback but it doesn't seem to be working? You've given repeated instances of feedback, and yet you don't see a change in a direct's behavior.

Many managers ask us this question because they're afraid that the relaxed tone and the lack of yelling, anger, punishment, and perceived consequences could lead directs to underestimate the manager's seriousness about the direct's need to change. They worry that the direct might say, "Yes, I'll change" but then not do so.

It's a reasonable concern, but it's not borne out by the facts. First, most of the managers who express this concern *haven't tried the model yet.* Here's what the data say: *Managers report to us that 91 percent of directs, when given negative feedback in our format, change their behavior after one instance.*

Before we talk about what to do, there is an important distinction to make here. We have to separate ineffective behaviors that would lead to negative feedback into two categories: different behaviors and similar behaviors. If one of your directs is making mistakes in several *different* areas of behavior, give them feedback in those different areas. Several instances of one mistake in different areas of behavior—say timeliness, quality, amount of work done, relationships with others, communication—isn't a problem (because of the 91 percent figure above).

But what if the behaviors are similar? What if someone is late repeatedly, even after you've given them negative feedback? What if someone fails to meet the quality standard two to three more times after you've given them feedback on their first miss?

Repeated behaviors without a change toward effectiveness are responded to by *Systemic Feedback*. It's easy to give—it's very similar to the four-step standard feedback model with a change in focus. If you already know how to give standard feedback, systemic feedback is simple to implement. But its simplicity belies its power. Really well-delivered systemic feedback is exceptionally hard to ignore and lays excellent groundwork for further efforts if the direct doesn't change his or her behavior.

Systemic feedback changes what you are talking to your direct about and raises the level of consequences associated with a continued failure to change. Systemic feedback addresses the direct's combination of continued failure to change with the direct's stated commitment to change. It addresses the greater failure to meet a repeated commitment. Failure to meet commitments is a systemic failure that no organization can long tolerate among its members.

It's best illustrated with an example. Suppose I have a direct who is struggling in an area. For this example, let's have it be the quality of his work. The standard for his insurance claim submissions is 98 percent on time, with less than 5 percent rejections due to errors or omissions. My direct has to turn materials in to an auditing team, and if it doesn't pass the quality audit, it comes back and he has to redo it.

Then I have to check it more thoroughly, which includes filling out a checklist that says I did look at it.

This direct's name is Austin. He's a good worker, sharp—I like him. But while he makes the deadline routinely, he also often misses the quality deadline.

Austin has good relationships with his teammates. He's well liked, has a degree (which is necessary for the career path he says he's interested in), and we agree that he has skills that would make him, at least in the beginning, a good supervisor. But not with this track record. He won't get promoted. *He's not performing well. He's not meeting one of his important job quality standards.*

So, when Austin fails to meet the standard, I give him some feedback.

It would probably have sounded like this:

Manager: Austin, can I share something with you?

Direct: Sure, boss.

Manager: When you fail to meet your quality goal—you're at 7 percent returns this week versus a standard of 5 percent, it means a lot more work for you and me. Can you work on that?

Direct: Sorry—yes I will.

Notice what happens here in the MT Feedback Model. I pointed out his mistake, told him the consequences, and asked him to change his behavior.

And he said he would. In step 4, we ask the direct to commit to changing his behavior.

Unfortunately, though, Austin continues to fail to meet his quality goal. And each week he fails, I give him negative feedback, and ask for his commitment to improve. He says yes. (This is not to say that I don't offer to help him, get him some training, find him a mentor, assist him myself—but those things are separate from my responsibility to give him feedback.)

When I'm giving this feedback week to week, *I'm not changing the tone or delivery in any way*. We don't escalate, or use a tone that suggests that "things are getting worse." We don't hint at consequences. Rest assured, our directs know that continued failure to change a behavior that we've asked to change is a problem.

I'm going to keep giving him feedback about his weekly failure for six weeks without much difference. I will probably offer him help, as mentioned above. But whether he accepts the help and uses it or doesn't, *I'm still obligated to give him the feedback*. I'm not going to not talk to him about his failure to meet a standard just because he's "working on it." I'm happy he's working on it, and I want him to continue. And, he's still not making it, and I'm still going to talk about that too.

Try not to let that six weeks figure worry you, for two reasons. First, using Systemic Feedback is incredibly rare. In 26 years of using a version of this Feedback Model, *I've only used systemic feedback six times*. That's once every four years, spread across what must be 100 directs at various times.

Second, if you suggest consequences are potentially forthcoming after one or two or even three instances, you're going to get some strong pushback. Directs who feel that they can't make a couple of mistakes—even in the same area—get defensive quickly. And relatedly, waiting gives them time to work on the problem, and it shows we trust them to get to where they need to be performance-wise.

Back to Austin. It's been seven weeks, so now I give him systemic feedback. Note how the focus changes.

Manager: "Austin, can I give you some feedback?"

Direct: "Sure." (He thinks he knows what's coming. What he *thinks* is coming is feedback about quality, which is not what he's going to get.)

Manager: "When you tell me week after week after week that you're going to improve your quality numbers and then you don't, my concern is no longer just about the quality of your work. It's about you making repeated commitments—to me—that you are failing to keep. In my mind, this is much more serious than missing your quality standard. Your word of commitment will follow you your entire career. What can you do differently about this more serious problem?"

Here is the fundamental difference. Standard feedback is about small behaviors. Systemic feedback addresses the moral hazard of a direct committing to new behavior but then failing to follow through. *We can tolerate directs who make mistakes. We* ***cannot*** *tolerate directs who repeatedly make commitments they don't keep.*

When Do We Use It?

You should use systemic feedback when you have already given six instances of standard feedback in a period of time that indicates a pattern, and the direct has not been engaging in the behavior they've committed to. This is the final step of feedback. You use systemic feedback before you think about considering organizational sanctions, like a performance improvement plan.

How Is It Different?

Systemic feedback is different from standard feedback because the behavior about which we're giving feedback is the failure to meet commitments (as opposed to the original behavior) that the direct agreed to in step 4 of the standard model when the direct said yes.

It perhaps feels different in that there is more of a sense of, "There could be consequences." Standard feedback is delivered lightly and professionally, without engaging in shows of power, anger, or fear, whereas systemic feedback is more serious. It is not appropriate to deliver systemic feedback in a casual way. Committing to actions and then not following through is notably more serious than missing a quality deadline, even if it is done repeatedly.

Two Dangers

Systemic feedback has two related dangers that we have to be cautious of.

1. *We Must Be Faithful to the Feedback Model's Step 4*. If we don't use the standard feedback model appropriately, we can't use the systemic feedback model. We have to have repeated commitments from our direct, which come out of step 4 ("Can you work on that?), to be able to address the direct's failure to keep the commitment.

   Perhaps the strongest motivation for most managers to use step 4 even when it feels awkward ("Really? I can't just point out their behavior? I have to ask for a change?") is that, without it, we are left with nowhere to go if the standard feedback model fails to change the direct's behavior.
2. *Implied Sanctions Must Be Delivered*. Because the systemic feedback is the last step in feedback, it's possible that some managers will throw up their hands in frustration at the direct's lack of change in behavior. I don't think that will be effective, but I understand the frustration.

What happens, then, is that we start to think about sanctions. Many managers have told us, "Feedback isn't working, so I'm going to put some teeth in it." That's perhaps not ideal, but it is reasonable after weeks and weeks of seeing no improvement.

However, if we promise sanctions, we must deliver them when and how we say they are going to be delivered, if behavior change is not forthcoming. If we promise to freeze the direct's salary for the next year, we had better freeze it. If we promise to remove the direct from the promotion interview list, we must do so. Otherwise, the direct will begin to see the entire process as a stalling tactic by us, and that will demotivate change going forward.

Systemic feedback is an exceptionally effective way to get the direct's attention and to motivate the change of a direct who has resisted change up to that point. It does so in a way that is faithful to the overall feedback system, which is all about behavior. It also adds weight to the delivery of the feedback, by addressing a far more dangerous behavioral weakness: a failure to meet commitments.

9

How to Start Delivering Feedback

STARTING TO DELIVER FEEDBACK FOLLOWS naturally after you've rolled out One On Ones. If, for some reason, you've jumped right to the feedback section of this book and you haven't rolled out your One On Ones yet, you could be in for a very rocky road. The guidance here doesn't address skipping One On Ones because we don't recommend things we don't believe in.

After 12 weeks of having One On Ones, you can start the process of delivering your performance communications in the Manager Tools Feedback Model.

Announce Your Intention in Your Weekly Staff Meeting

Now that you've decided to begin adding feedback to your Manager Tools and you've been developing better relationships with your directs, you've got to announce your intended change to your team all at once. Feedback is an individual behavior, but announcing it to the team says that everyone is going to treated similarly. We don't recommend giving the same briefing over and over again in your One On Ones—that's inefficient.

141

Schedule 30 Minutes for Your Briefing

We've seen managers try to shoehorn the meeting into 10 to 15 minutes, but that's usually not enough time. With directs' sensitivities about performance communications, it's better to not rush.

Use Our Materials

We've got a free feedback document on our website that gives you everything you need. Hand it out to your directs. It will make it much easier for them to receive feedback if they know what's coming and why it's coming.

Cover the Purpose of Feedback

Talk to your directs about the purpose of giving feedback, which is to "encourage effective future behavior." Unfortunately, there have been too many bad bosses over the years. The fear that your directs will feel about feedback will cause them to attribute to you motives that you are unlikely to have in your heart. So, you've got to counteract that fear and tell them plainly why you're using the feedback model.

Tell them when you give them feedback, you're focused on the future. When you have to give them negative feedback, tell them you'll do your best to be relaxed and not accusatory. Tell them you know there's nothing we can do about a mistake that's in the past, so there's no sense getting upset after the fact.

Walk Them through Each Step of the Feedback Model

Tell your directs what you're going to do and how you're going to do it. Talk about each step. Practice with them. Ask *them* for examples of positive feedback, and do your best to show them how you're going to use the feedback model.

Here's one way to share with your directs why you're thinking of using this tool. "I've got an obligation to help you be at your very best every day. If you're like me, you're not always sure that your good work is being recognized or that it's what the boss wants. And you're not sure if you're always doing it exactly right or if there is a better way to do it. The feedback model is just a way for us to talk about what you're doing and what the results are."

Tell your directs that negative feedback isn't about punishment; it's about doing things better. It is about the future.

Give Only Positive Feedback for Eight Weeks

Don't give *any* negative feedback as you're learning to use the feedback model. If you try to slip in some negative feedback, you run the risk of doing it poorly because you haven't yet mastered the model and the delivery. You may hurt the feelings of your direct. Now you've "poisoned the well" of the model, and even if later you give that direct some positive feedback, the direct's dislike of the model will make it difficult to hear your praise.

It's likely that even though you tell your directs that you *will only be giving positive feedback using the model for the next eight weeks*, the first time you ask a direct, "Can I give you some feedback?" you'll see some panic or fear. That should tell you how directs have been treated by their previous managers. They've learned to be afraid of any performance communications, because they are rare and so often negative.

If you are wondering how much feedback you should give, shoot for one item of feedback to one direct per day as you start. This does not mean one item of feedback to *each of your directs* but, rather, just one item of feedback to *any one* member of your team. Start slowly.

If you can go five days in a row having given feedback one time, raise your limit to two, and so on. [There's a Cast for That™—It's called Measuring Feedback.]

What should you do if one of your directs makes a mistake that is worthy of some negative feedback before it's time for you to roll out negative feedback? Do whatever you did before you knew about the model. If you ignored the problem before, ignore it again. If you yelled, you could probably even get away with yelling (but I wish you wouldn't). Even though you have this new tool, and you may even be a little excited about using it, don't use it before it's time in the rollout process. If you normally would take them into your office for a chat, do that.

Add in Negative Feedback after Eight Weeks

Notice that we don't "switch" from positive to negative feedback. We just start looking for opportunities to give negative as well as positive feedback. We recommend you wait because you need to learn the model well before you start using it to give negative feedback. You don't want to be awkward or clumsy if there's a chance it will make the moment less useful or more stressful with your directs.

Stay as Positive as You Can

Be careful that you don't overdo negative feedback. Most managers fail to realize how much they see their job as "correcting mistakes." If you believe you should be "vigilant" against "mistakes," two things will happen gradually: you'll start seeing all the mistakes, and you'll stop seeing all the good behaviors.

Great managers will tell you that they give out far more positive than negative performance communications. They look for opportunities to point out things that are going well. If they didn't, they probably wouldn't have noticed them. And, whether you like it or not, in an organization full of humans, there are going to be a lot of mistakes. Even if you think of yourself as good at policing mistakes, many, many more happen than you will ever see.

Positive feedback is a much more powerful tool than negative feedback. Don't wait your entire career to finally realize that.

10

Ask for More—Coaching

THE THIRD CRITICAL BEHAVIOR FOR effective managers is to ask for higher levels of performance: Ask for More. The Manager Tools Coaching Model allows you to help each of your directs grow their skills without you spending more than 5–10 minutes a week on their improvement efforts.

Most managers with some experience have been in at least one situation in which they knew they needed to help someone grow. One of their colleagues, or someone from HR probably said, "You really need to coach him." Maybe one of their directs was performing reasonably well, but needed help in one skill area to get to the next level. Or, a direct was struggling enough that their future was in jeopardy.

But no one knew how. Or, it involved weeks and weeks of developing a detailed six-month improvement plan (which no one else had ever done before). So, they let it gather dust on the back of their desk, and never got to it.

But there's a better way. And there needs to be, because we're obligated as managers to get the most out of our directs as we can. If a direct is capable of more/better/higher performance, the manager is obligated to work hard to make it happen.

Coaching is the least often used tool in the "Management Trinity." There are some good reasons for this. One On Ones are the most powerful tool, and once managers start having O3s they never want to let them go. Feedback happens next, but it's hard for many managers, so they stumble. Many managers are afraid of introducing conflict, fearing it may increase turnover rates (even though, of course, the opposite is the case). If managers can't get through feedback, it's unlikely they're going to embrace coaching. Feedback takes seconds, but coaching takes months—it seems much harder.

We offer an important caveat here about vocabulary: *coaching*, in different parts of the professional world, has two different meanings. In some cases, it just means a manager pointing out mistakes and making suggestions—very episodic, very ad hoc. Nothing systemic, nothing planned. (And by the way: it's always negative.)

There's also a large number of organizations where coaching is really one name given to the "Performance Improvement Plan" that a failing employee is put on. The employee is not put on the plan to succeed but, rather, to allow the organization to gather objective data about the employee's failure to perform to give them enough data to terminate employment without legal risk.

Manager Tools defines coaching as a systemic effort to improve the performance of a direct in a specific skill area. It's neither episodic nor inherently negative. Our Coaching Model is a way for you to supervise the self-improvement process of one of your directs, over a series of months.

Our Coaching Model has four simple steps:
Step 1: Collaborate to Set a Goal
Step 2: Collaborate to Brainstorm Resources
Step 3: Collaborate to Create a Plan
Step 4: The Direct Acts and Reports on the Plan

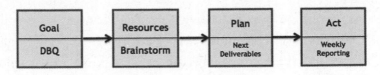

Figure 10.1   Coaching Model

Step 1: Collaborate to Set a Goal

The first step is really simple. Once we've decided what our direct is going to get better at—more about which in a moment—we sit down with the direct and set a goal.

Note that the first three steps of our model start with the word *collaborate*. We sit down with the direct and set goals, brainstorm resources, and create a set of action steps that we call a coaching plan. Only in step 4, when the direct takes actions in the plan while we monitor the direct's actions, do our paths diverge, and then it's only slightly.

Coaching is most effective when it is collaborative. Managers know where the most likely opportunities are, but the direct is the one who will be learning and growing, and the manager can't do that for the direct any more than the direct can always be right picking the topic or knowing the resources.

How do we set a goal? Easy. We describe a behavior or a result that we want to achieve by a date when we want it achieved. Here are some examples:

- By 1 December, you will attain Certified Network Engineer (CNE) status.
- By 30 October, you will run the staff meeting successfully.
- By 1 January, you will submit the Capital Plan without errors

Manager Tools uses a goal structure called DBQ: Deadline, Behavior, Quality. We start with the Deadline portion because deadlines drive behavior. Also, because we remember that coaching is a more powerful tool than feedback, we usually don't set deadlines of less than four months away. If someone can change their behavior in less than four months, the person probably just needs a lot of feedback and we don't need a coaching plan.

The Behavior portion is what we want the direct to master—the behavior we want to improve.

The Quality portion is how we're going to measure the behavior. For instance, we can't just say we're going to have a direct run a meeting, if that's what we're working on. Under that criterion, the direct could run a meeting that was disastrous. We have to define *what the measure of success is* for the behavior we're expecting to change.

We recommend you write down the coaching engagement goal on your One-On-One forms. Many of us do it on the back of the previous week's form, and only coaching notes go there, so we can always keep them separate.

It helps audiences we train to learn about the Manager Tools Coaching Model through an example. Let's take one that surprises a lot of managers: coaching one of our directs who has a problem interrupting people. This is the kind of example most managers assume "can't be done" because "you can't coach interpersonal skills." But since interpersonal skills are just behaviors, we can.

Our direct's name is Derek. Our coaching collaboration with him might have started like this:

"Derek, I'm concerned that you haven't reduced your interruptions. I've given you several instances of feedback about it, and I've not seen you make much, if any, change. I feel your interrupting is a behavior we can and should reduce, and that will make some difference in improving your relationships among the team. Interruptions hurt others' perceptions of your respect for them. They assume that when you interrupt them as often as you do, you don't respect them very much."

Now: how do we apply a DBQ goal to Derek's plan?

For a deadline, four months would bring us roughly to 1 January. We're not going to have a deadline during the holiday season, and, frankly, what's wrong with thinking he might need more than four months, so let's give him six months. It's far better for us to overestimate and have Derek finish early than to have him be stressed out about a deadline that we would probably let slip a little bit anyway. So, our deadline is going to be 1 March. We start therefore with "By 1 March . . ."

Now, what behavior are we working on, and how are we going to measure it? That's easy: interruptions, or the absence of interruptions. We want an event, a measurable, short time span during which we're basically going to sample Derek's behavior and measure it against a standard.

Let's try this: "By 1 March, you will go through an entire weekly operations meeting without making a single interruption."

Notice that we say "try" here. There is no one approved solution to how to help any person get better at any skill or ability. Too many of us managers mistakenly think, "Oh, there's a right way to do this, but since I don't know it, and there's risk in being wrong, it's better not to try." Rather than making the perfect the enemy of the good, we're going to take some steps to help Derek. *If they don't work perfectly, we don't care, as long as Derek makes progress that he wouldn't have made had we not tried.*

As we think further about Derek, it occurs to us that one way he can reduce his interrupting is to simply not talk. That's obviously not a good solution, because he's going to have to talk to get his work done, and if during the sample period Derek doesn't talk, that really won't be an indication of him having gotten a handle on his habit of interrupting. So, we'll have to add some sort of measure in our goal to address this potential gaming of the system.

We end up with this: "By 1 March, you will go through an entire weekly operations meeting without making a single interruption, while contributing something at least five times. How does that sound, Derek? Do you feel we can get there—that it's reasonable and achievable?" There also wouldn't be anything wrong with determining in the first month of our work on this that Derek averages seven to nine contributions in an operations meeting, and then changing the Quality measurement.

Step 2: Collaborate to Brainstorm Resources

Now we have a goal, but how do we get there? If you're thinking you wouldn't know what to do in this situation, you're not alone, but you're also giving yourself too little credit. *You don't have to know how to get someone from start to finish to stop interrupting. You only have to know how to start them to learn how to not interrupt.*

We get to the goal by jointly brainstorming the resources that the direct could use to become more effective at the skill on which we're coaching him. Part of our coaching plan will include finding out what resources are available and availing ourselves of them without even knowing which one is best. If we don't do it this way, then every manager will be limited to coaching on what he or she knows and is confident coaching others on. This would mean that there would be exceptionally limited coaching opportunities for both managers and directs, and suddenly the organization would be limited enormously in how it could grow and what it would become.

It would be okay in a Manager Tools coaching engagement to have a task of reading a book which might be helpful but actually proved not to be helpful. You could say that time was "wasted" on reading that book, and in a way you'd be right. But to avoid doing anything that might be wrong, what most of us do is nothing at all.

This is a hard concept for most managers to grasp. We all seem to want silver bullets—quick and easy, one-shot, no-brainer solutions. Stop looking for those (there aren't any). Start thinking about things that might work. When they do, celebrate the progress toward the goal. When they don't, consider it a lesson learned. (Perhaps this point alone makes it understandable why we added a couple of extra months to the DBQ deadline. We're not delivering a product here against a strict delivery deadline. We're helping someone improve.)

How do we brainstorm resources? We sit down with our direct and brainstorm. If you're like me and Wendii, we do so over the phone. We follow the brainstorm guidance that we have in our podcast on that topic [There's a Cast for That™], and we take two to three minutes to come up with a list of potential resources that we think might be potentially helpful to our direct in learning and doing this new or better skill.

Suppose you were coaching a direct on improving their meeting management techniques, for instance, as indicated in our goal example above. You might list the following: Google, Toastmasters, Manager Tools, Amazon, Dale Carnegie, fellow managers, executives, Robert's Rules of Order, podcasts, *Meetings for Dummies*, meeting videotapes, agenda training, and so on.

The idea with all brainstorming is simply to go for volume, not accuracy. This again runs counter to what a lot of managers want—a silver bullet—which, of course, doesn't exist. We're not looking for the *one* right thing. We're looking for lots of possible things, hoping that out of all of them there will probably be one to five things that will collectively get us where we need to go. It is silly for us to assume we will know exactly how to improve someone else in some skill that we ourselves are not necessarily good at.

So, we take a couple of minutes and write down everything we think of in our brainstorming session. Maybe one item sticks out, maybe another doesn't. In brainstorming, anything goes, including peanut butter. Whether we use any one of the ideas or resources is saved for step 3.

Table 10.1 is a list that we created in one minute to coach someone on the habit of interrupting:

TABLE 10.1   List for Coaching Someone on The Habit of Interrupting

Tannen Book	Vanderbilt book	Amazon
Notify team	Private coach	Google
Books	Predetermined rewards	Blogs
Weekly reporting	Physical cheat	Weekly check-ins
Apology required	Interpersonal skills class	Charm school
Stopwatch	YouTube videos	Podcasts
Charm coach	Self-reporting	Manager Tools Forums
Peanut butter	Influence book	Cadet hostesses

Step 3: Collaborate to Create a Plan

We've got a goal, we've got a pile of ideas to get us there; what now? Now we just create *the first few weeks of a plan*—a series of steps that Derek will take, to help him start learning and improving his behavior. We can either use one resource, if we agree that it's a great one to use and is free, or we can use two to three together. We could, perhaps, use one resource (for example, visiting other meetings for a few days) until we can use the book we ordered from Amazon about meetings: *Meetings for Dummies*.

The steps in the plan each have three parts: a deadline, a behavior, and the reporting that the task is done, which is inherent in the task. The reporting (see the list below) is what makes a task a *deliverable*.

Here are some examples of tasks from a different plan, showing each of the three parts.

■ By 15 July, e-mail me a receipt for your order of the book *The Effective Executive* from Amazon.

- By 7 May, send me an e-mail on what you have learned listening to Manager Tools Podcast on Pre-Wire.
- By 19 March, send me an e-mail with names of three potential mentors.

We want to let our direct have significant input in the resources we create tasks for, because he will be the one doing the work. Don't expect the direct to learn it the way we did. Mike likes to read books; I like having mentors. Neither one is right; they're just different. This is just respect for behavioral diversity.

Now let's return to our example of Derek. Let's say that Derek really likes to attend classes. That's fine. We might have some money in the training budget to do that. But we recommend that you start with lower-cost things, like a book, a mentor, a podcast, or reading a blog. There's nothing wrong with picking two resources: one that Derek wants and one that you want, presumably because you have some idea of what might work best, and Derek knows what might work best for him.

Note here something that surprises a lot of managers: we're only going to plan the first one to two weeks. We are not going to plan the entire six months' worth of work. It will take too long, we don't know enough, and things will change 10 times between now and then. We'll never coach anyone with that model of full planning.

Before we start creating deliverables from resources, though, I want you to learn to think differently about task creation and assignment. (We do this at all of our 100+ Effective Manager Training conferences every year.) Think about you and your team of directs. Suppose you assigned each member of your team a specific, relevant professional development book to read, and gave them a month to read it. (Assume it's short enough that it wouldn't be burdensome). Tell them that you want them to read it, and then sit down as a group with you at the end of the month and talk about what they learned. You are not going to supply the book, but you'll reimburse them for buying it themselves (and it's readily available). You trust them to have read it and you'll let them do it at their own pace, as long as they're ready to discuss it at the end of the month.

Now answer this question with a yes or no: *would half of your team have finished the book by the end of the month and be able to discuss it?*

At our conferences, out of 30 attendees, maybe five raise their hands indicating yes.

If you're like most managers, you've learned that if you assign additional work, and give it a long deadline, it's unlikely to get done. That's what we've learned when it comes to coaching directs. Even when their development is *necessary* (because they're underperforming), the vast majority of directs struggle with long deadlines. Lots of managers see it as a way to trust their directs, to not micromanage them. Even with those noble intentions, it doesn't make any sense to do this *when we know it doesn't work.*

And it's not just that 30-day-long tasks are problematic. They're the worst of offenders, but they're not the only one. We've also found that, if we assign tasks of as long as a week and we check each week, urgent daily activities regularly take precedence, leading to coaching "projects" being behind by a week immediately, and then additional weeks as each new week passes.

And at some level you know that urgency is a key driver of organizational behavior. You know that, if you have to do something and there's no deadline, all other things being equal, you're going to act on the tasks that have deadlines that are reportable or enforceable, and you won't do the one that has no deadline.

What we've learned in the past 25 years, studying thousands of coaching cases, is the best way to help people improve is by creating short-term tasks.

Deadlines that are going to be enforced but that are believed to be reasonable and reachable are a big facilitator of coaching success. You don't need clever learning techniques, or special budgeting, or someone to analyze your direct's learning style. Reachable and reasonable deadlines drive behavior better than anything else.

So, what the Manager Tools Coaching Tool does is leverage what we know of human organizational behavior to set short deadlines, on do-able tasks, to increase the chance of completion.

Here's an example of how we might go about considering or even hiring a personal coach, which was one of the resources listed in Table 10.1.

- By 3 PM today, Monday, send me a list of five books on Amazon that deal with communications, habits, or interrupting that you think might be helpful.
- By 11 AM Tuesday morning, e-mail me a receipt for the book you ordered.
- By noon Thursday, e-mail me a picture of the book on your desk.
- By 3 PM Friday, send me a three sentence overview of Chapter 1 of the book you bought.

You can probably imagine what Monday's deliverable will be. Before you overreact and call this micromanaging: it's not. It's managing. It's encouraging effective behaviors to get results. And at the end of this week, Derek will have read the first chapter of the book, while the vast majority of managers can't be sure even half their team will read the book *in a month*.

By tightening tasks down to in some cases almost an hourly scope, we can, in the first week, start reading a book. We will also have helped Derek feel like he's getting somewhere: he has completed several deliverables, all on time. He doesn't start out dreading a month long task he's constantly putting off. He starts out in our next O3 saying he accomplished all five tasks he agreed to.

This feeling of accomplishment is not to be taken lightly. It will lead to more effort in the weeks ahead, more willingness to keep at the self-improvement project when there are other tasks on the direct's desk.

Also notice the use of tasks that are not done until they are reported on as "being done." Yes, work is "done" in the mind of the doer when she finishes the task, but the work has no value to the organization until the organization knows it's done. That's the difference between assigning a task and assigning a deliverable. [There's a Cast for That™.]

Further, think for a second about a direct who has finished a task and the manager who doesn't yet know the task is done. In order for other work to be done, assigned, or aggregated, the manager needs to know that the first task has been done. It is done, but the manager doesn't know it yet. At this point, who is the best person to help the manager know it is done?

The answer is the direct, for two reasons. First, the direct is the first to know, and reporting is always easier for the one who did the work. Second, the direct can do the report on it in less time than the manager can find out that it's done, at a lower labor cost per minute, too.

Thus, we don't assign reading a chapter of a book, for instance. We assign the task of reporting (to the boss) that reading.

There's something else that's important here as well. The adult learning model reminds us that we learn by doing. Whenever possible, we look for opportunities to observe our direct engaging in the behavior we want, to provide the direct with feedback on what we observe, and we make that a regular, very short-scope task.

We cannot stress this enough. All the classes in the world, all the books, all the mentors—none of that matters if the behavior doesn't change. When it comes to interpersonal behavior—in this case, interrupting—our direct will have many chances to do well or stumble every day and every week.

In this scenario, assigning deliverables that enable the manager to view the behavior being coached might look like this:

- Achieve two or fewer interruptions in your interactions with me, in all of our interactions this week.
- Achieve one or zero interruption in your interactions with me, in all of our interactions this week.
- Achieve no interruptions in your interactions with me, in all of our interactions this week.

We might assign the first task in weeks 1–5, the second task in weeks 6–10, and so on. Further, these tasks, because they involve us as manager, don't require reporting along with the task. They are inherently deliverables because the task happens with the person being reported to (the manager).

Step 4: The Direct Acts and Reports on the Plan

Step 4 is the step that carries us through the rest of the effort. Once we collaborate on a goal and collaborate on resources, we collaborate on some very short-scope tasks, and then the direct gets to work.

The way this process is set up, we're getting daily or at least regular updates in the form of task completion e-mails, and we are briefly discussing the direct's progress each week during our One On One. If we are coaching one of our directs, we expect the direct to brief us during the One On One on his or her progress for the week. As a general rule, we wait until the end of the O3. We don't tell the direct to spend the direct's time on the agenda updating us. We tell the direct that we'll ask about it during our agenda time, or we'll cover it in the "future" portion of the O3.

Every week, in every One On One, we're reviewing completed tasks, rescheduling uncompleted tasks, and creating new deliverables based on where we are in the process. That may include going back to our brainstormed resource list.

What do we do if the direct doesn't accomplish all of the tasks? What do we do when the direct runs out of tasks?

When They Fail to Accomplish Something the Previous Week

If the direct fails to accomplish something the previous week, we give the direct negative feedback. Here is an example:

Manager: "Derek, can I give you some feedback?"
Direct: "Sure."
Manager: "When you miss your coaching deadlines, that's more work for later. Can you change that?"
Direct: "Sure, I'll do better."

Manager: "Can I give you some feedback?"
Direct: "Yes."
Manager: "When you don't meet with your mentor, I worry about your motivation to get better."
Direct: "You're right, boss. I'll get back on track."

Manager: "Can I give you some feedback?"
Direct: "Of course."
Manager: "When you don't let me know the task is done, I don't get a sense of how you're doing."
Direct: "Thanks, boss."

Manager: "Derek, can I give you some feedback?"
Direct: "Of course."

Manager: "When you interrupt twice during our staff meeting, it slows down your progress."
Direct: "Thanks and I'll work harder."

Conversely, why not give Derek positive feedback for the deliverables he did achieve? See if you can work out how one of those might sound, for some of the deliverables we created above.

When They Run Out of Tasks

Very short-scope planning means you're back to planning the next week or two very quickly. Many managers are surprised when the five to ten very short-scope tasks that they assigned in the first week are already done within that first week, or even a day or two. (Yes, some do complain, wanting to go back to assigning month-long tasks, which they know don't work but are much easier to manage.)

When the direct runs out of tasks, we just sit down in the next O3 and either extend the resource the direct is already using (more mentor meetings, more book chapters to read, more meetings to attend during which interruptions are counted, more positive feedback goals on not interrupting) or go back to our resource list to see if there's something there we could use to help the direct move toward the goal.

When a particular resource doesn't seem to work, we stop using it. This is particularly important to remember when we and our direct are different in style or behavioral tendency. If you're a perfectionist and your direct is a high energy sales type, don't force the direct to read five more books. Let your direct get a mentor, or a buddy, or attend a seminar, for instance.

That's the Manager Tools Coaching Model, with a detailed example. In the next chapter, we'll walk through rolling it out.

11

How to Start Coaching

FOLLOWING 12 WEEKS OF ONE On Ones, and eight weeks of only positive feedback, followed by eight weeks of both positive and negative feedback, it's time to roll out coaching slowly. Set aside time in your weekly staff meeting, and walk through the four-step Manager Tools Coaching Model. If you have time, give your directs examples of Deadline, Behavior, Quality (DBQ) goals and of how effective tasks are actually deliverables with short deadlines.

You've introduced and started One On Ones after three weeks. You've started giving positive feedback after 12 weeks of having One On Ones, and then you waited eight more weeks to start giving negative feedback.

Eight weeks after that, start coaching one or two top performers. We are now 31 weeks into the rollout process. *That's roughly eight months.*

It's not a good idea to try to start coaching everyone all at once. Even though it doesn't take as much time as One On Ones, coaching feels more intensive to many managers. It will be more fun to coach a top performer because you probably won't feel that it's a "must improve" situation the way you will feel as you start to coach some of your at-risk performers.

After coaching a couple of your top performers through one or two successful coaching sessions, roll out coaching more broadly across your entire team.

12

Push Work Down—Delegation

DELEGATION IS ONE OF THE core reasons my Manager Tools cofounder Mike Auzenne did so well as an executive. He recognized early as a software development manager that his job had changed from solving technical problems to making others more effective so they could solve problems. His job had changed from one about technology to one about people. When he continued to get promoted, he realized that his job had changed again—from leveraging others' technical skills to leveraging others' people skills. And he found that if he hired or promoted the right people, he could trust them to take on more and more responsibility. And he delegated more and more responsibilities to them over time to help them grow.

Mike realized he individually was able to do more because he himself had been trusted with more to do along the way. He benefited enormously from his bosses giving him more to do.

Learning to delegate is part of the transition to becoming an executive. Too many managers today think that because they are smarter and more effective at getting things done than their directs, they should try to get more done by doing it themselves. This isn't sustainable, and I've seen the failure scenario play out a hundred times. An up and coming manager does more and more *themselves* (likely working ever longer hours) and gets a reputation as someone who gets things done. Finally they get what they think of as "the big promotion"—to the executive level. And two years later, they "resign to pursue other opportunities."

What happened? They didn't learn to trust their folks and delegate as a manager. Then, when they got that "big" promotion, their workload *tripled*. What's more, as an executive, they had to spend roughly a third of their time talking to other execs, building coalitions to get things done.

So now, their workload has tripled, and their time to get it done has been cut by a third. And they haven't developed a trusted set of managers in their organization that they can delegate to, nor do they know how. And, they drown in the new job they were desperate to get. And they are *asked* to resign in lieu of being fired, because firing executives looks bad.

If you're a manager, your key to long-term success is to master the art of delegation.

Before we turn to the why's and how's of delegation, though, we need to make an important distinction about what delegation is and what it isn't. Just because work passes between you and your direct doesn't make it delegation. It might be a simple task assignment.

How do we know when something is a task assignment and not a delegation? Here's an example of what would be a task assignment. Assume you're a software development manager. You manage a team of people who write software code for an industrial firm. One of the groups you support is the production floor. The VP of production often asks for your team to support something he's doing.

The VP comes to you one day and says, "We've got a new robot that we need some code written for. Can you have it done by the end of the week?" When you agree, you've accepted a new responsibility. But this responsibility is coming to you in your role as the leader of the software development team. Your role as the leader means that you're the clearinghouse for who gets assigned what on your team (generally). You're not delegating a task when it's not a task you would normally do, and you're simply assigning that task among members of your team. This is an example of task assignment.

Delegation, on the other hand, is you turning over responsibility for one of your regular responsibilities—something you routinely do—on a permanent or long standing basis, to one of your directs.

Task assignment is different from delegation. [There's a Cast For That™.]

Why Delegation Is the Solution—The Delegation Cascade

I'd like to walk you through a workload management scenario that we often share with managers who attend our Effective Manager Conferences. You're a manager with five directs. The diagram that follows represents your weekly managerial workload (see Figure 12.1). The box itself represents your 50-hour work week. Think of it as "holding" 50 hours' worth of work. (I know you may work more or less than that, but allow me to simplify things a little.) Each ball in the box represents one of your responsibilities— something that you spend time on each week. You'll note that there are five big balls and 15 small balls—a total of 20 balls. And, for simplicity's sake, we're going to assume that everyone in your organization has 20 balls in their box, and everyone works 50 hours

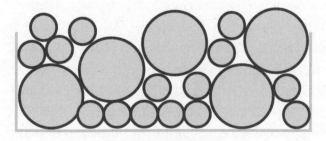

Figure 12.1   Work Life Diagram: 20 Balls

a week. Of course, this isn't exactly true, but it's a reasonable way to model an organization for a workload discussion.

Each of the big balls in the box represents one of your core responsibilities. You obviously spend more time on your core responsibilities, so they take up more space in your 50-hour week. Further, we're going to assume that you spend *five times* longer working on any one of your most important responsibilities than you do on any one of your smaller responsibilities. (It isn't always true that everyone spends more time on their biggest responsibilities, but it should be.) The size of the balls in the box connotes both their importance and the amount of time you spend on them.

You'll also note that the box is full. It's pretty clear you couldn't fit another ball into the box. But of course, that's true, right? We are all always telling everyone we meet how busy we are, how we don't have time to do more, and so on.

You might think that you could get more out of your week if you could fill up some of those empty spaces between the balls with work. But that's not really possible. You have to eat lunch most days, you have to use the restroom, you have to take mental breaks throughout the day, you probably talk/text your family one or two times a day, and sometimes you spend 15 minutes on the Internet, checking sports scores. *There's no way you're ever going to be 100 percent efficient.* The in-between spaces represent our natural inefficiencies. Nothing wrong with making them a little smaller, but they're never going to go away.

But suddenly, things get interesting. While you're sitting at your desk, coping with the 20 balls you've got, your boss, the VP, asks you to take over responsibility for something she's been working on. The reason she does this is that the CEO has just taken on responsibility for a huge new client, and has pushed some responsibilities down to the chief operating officer (COO), who has done the same thing to your boss, the VP. And she's doing the same to you.

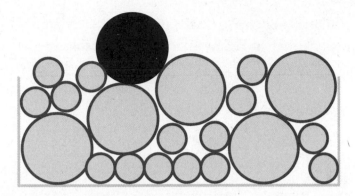

Figure 12.2   Work Life Diagram: 21 Balls

You immediately realize this is going to take you a bunch of time to get done—it's not just any ball, it's a big ball.

Suddenly, you've got 21 balls, and now not five but six of them are big (see Figure 12.2). And there's not room in your existing workweek for this new workload. Your box, your professional day-to-day life, is now out of stasis. You're going to have to make a change.

Before you start finding solutions to this problem, there are some constraints. You cannot work more hours. The size of the box is the absolute maximum your spouse or body will allow you to work. You could work more hours for a short period, but this isn't a responsibility you can dispatch in a couple of all-nighters. This is a new, permanent part of your job and responsibilities. Your boss used to do it, which means it matters.

You can't work "smarter." Over time, we all get smarter about our work, and we all can do more, but that isn't the solution in this case. You can't instantly get smart enough to be able to do the work required for the new ball, too. Nor can you suddenly/immediately get a lot better at doing the rest of your responsibilities (the rest of the balls).

And finally, you can't say no. You've told your boss you want more responsibility. It wouldn't be smart for you to turn down what you've been asking for.

The solution, of course, is *delegation*.

If you look back at Figure 12.2, you can see that you have three choices:

Delegate the big black ball.

Delegate one of the big gray balls.

Delegate one or more of the small gray balls.

Let's take these three options in order.

Delegate the Big Black Ball

Delegating your new responsibility, the big black ball, is *an extremely bad idea*. Why? In part because *you don't know how to do it yet*. If you don't know how to do it, how are you going to help your direct to whom you delegate it learn how to do it? How are you going to know if the direct is following the right path? Are you going to refer all their questions to your boss? You need to understand the work (remember, you've never done it before) before you can delegate it.

Don't ever delegate a new responsibility your boss has just given you to one of your directs. Learn it first, master it, before you consider delegating it.

Delegate One of the Big Gray Balls

At first glance, this seems like a reasonable answer. If you're going to have to delegate something, why not delegate a single item—it involves less hassle, right? There's only one problem with that. Let's imagine that your directs have a box, just like yours. Their time is restricted by their spouse or their bodies. They also already have 20 projects for which they are responsible.

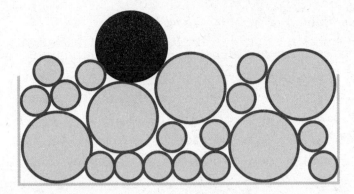

Figure 12.3   Delegate One of Your Small Balls

What does it look like when you delegate one of your small balls to one of your directs? Look at Figure 12.3.

Just in case you didn't get it, we'll say it again. *This is what it looks like when you delegate one of your SMALL balls to one of your directs.*

One of your small balls is a big ball to your direct.

The direct doesn't know how to do the task, and the expectations are higher. It's tough. They have to spend more time to get it done. And because it was something you used to do, by definition it's going to be as important as any of the big balls they're already working/spending time on.

Why shouldn't you delegate one of your big balls to your direct? Because it would get bigger, and it would crush him. Because the balls get bigger as they go down the organizational hierarchy, your directs will be overwhelmed.

If you thought about splitting a big ball among multiple directs, that's generally not a good plan, either. We've tested it. If it were easy to split the ball, the ball probably would have already been split up into smaller balls. Plus, you'll end up spending more time than you realize coordinating all the work that you split up, so you don't get as much time savings as you want/need.

Delegate One or More of the Small Balls

Since we've eliminated all the other options, this must be the right answer. Let's look at Figure 12.1 again. Assume that five small balls are equal in size to one big ball. So, in order to have enough time for you to do the work required for that big black ball that your boss just gave you, you'll need to delegate five of your small balls.

The best solution is to delegate each of the five small balls to a different direct. And now you are part of an important organizational behavior pattern that helps good organizations become great.

The CEO comes in with his new customer, and as a result, he delegates one of his responsibilities to the COO. The COO delegates one of his responsibilities to your VP. The VP delegates one of her responsibilities to you. This rolls down the organization. And it's called The Delegation Cascade.

At many conferences we present, at this point, we're interrupted. There's a flaw in our reasoning, we're told. "The model 'breaks' when you get to the lowest level, because the individual contributor who reports to the frontline manager doesn't have anyone to delegate to. She's going to get crushed!"

Not at all. *The individual contributor stops doing something* (or, more specifically, and to stay with the math, five small things). We call this "delegating to the floor."

"Wait," you say. "The individual contributor can't just stop doing things." Well, actually, she can. For the organization, the choice is between the CEO accepting a new customer account worth millions, or not, and having to delegate something, and a direct at the lowest level of the organization not setting aside something that is trivial compared to that new customer. If we're going to protect everything that individual contributor does, we're going to force the company to stop taking on new customers, new revenue, new opportunities in the marketplace. All because "everybody's busy."

Surely not.

Yes, this example is simplified a little. But rest assured, this is what the CEO expects to happen throughout his or her organization. And, there's more to the decision that individual contributor has to make about what they might "delegate to the floor." [And, as you might imagine, There's a Cast For That™.]

How to Delegate—The Manager Tools Delegation Model

So now that we know why we need to delegate, we need to know how to delegate. Once you've decided to delegate to a direct, the actual delegation is relatively easy. The initial conversation will take very little time and can take place in a One On One or at another convenient time. Delegating has five steps.

1. State your desire for help
2. Tell them why you're asking *them*
3. Ask for specific acceptance
4. Describe the task or project in detail
5. Address deadline, quality, and reporting standards

1. State Your Desire for Help

It's simple. "Sarah, I'd like your help." When we ask managers at our conferences, "How many of you, if your boss asked for help, would say yes, without needing to know any details?" Ninety percent of the managers say yes. Just asking for help almost guarantees you that you're going to be able to delegate the activity to your direct.

Notice, we don't say, "Brian, can you do me a favor?" This isn't a personal request. It's a work request. We're asking nicely, but we're not getting personal.

We also don't say, "Sarah, I need some help." That word "need" gives the direct the impression that they don't have a choice. But the best delegations allow the direct to say no.

2. Tell Them Why You're Asking Them

You say, as an example, "You're my best writer." We're not cozying up to Sarah here; we're trying to help her understand our rationale for choosing her. We didn't just pluck this assignment out of thin air. We want Sarah to know that we thought about it carefully and believe she is the right person for the job.

How can you know which of your directs is right for this responsibility? There's a simple guideline you can apply that will help. (We're assuming here that you've spent time getting to know your directs' strengths and weaknesses and won't have any problems with this.)

Look for four areas of your directs' abilities to determine what to delegate to whom: what they're *good* at, what they *like* to do, what they *need* to do, or what they *want* to do. As a general rule, disregard what *you* are good at, or what you *like* to do. This isn't about you. In delegating your lesser responsibilities, you ought not to be thinking about yourself. They're not valuable to you, but they could be very valuable to your directs. *Don't think about you, and about what you want to get rid of. Think about them, and what they could benefit from.*

1. **What they're good at:** If your direct is good at something, *even if you are too, delegate to their strengths.* Don't not delegate something because you're good at it. Trust them with it. Because you're good, you'll be a good resource for them.
2. **What they like to do:** If they have an affinity for an area, whether they're good at it or not, consider delegating in that area to them. Don't hold on to something you like because you like it. If they like it, let it go. Even better if you can delegate something you don't like to someone who does like it. When you love doing something, it tells you all its secrets.

3. **What they *need* to do.** If you have a direct who needs to improve in a skill area (often for consideration for promotions or career choices), delegate in this skill area to help them get there. The adult learning model says the best way to learn is to do.

4. **What they *want* to do.** If a direct has a desire in a certain area, delegate to them in that area. Even if you have a similar desire, for your smaller responsibilities, you're unlikely to be getting a lot out of it. Help them grow by giving them what they say they want, when possible.

3. Ask for Specific Acceptance

We ask our direct to accept the responsibility before we tell them the details of what's involved. Before you get too surprised, ask yourself: would you ever delegate something to one of your directs that they couldn't do? Something that would crush them? Of course you wouldn't. You might want them to stretch, but surely you care enough about them to never ask them to do anything that would be too much.

We say, "Would you please take over writing my monthly operations report?" Many people are surprised here. We don't give Sarah all the details before we ask for acceptance. We ask for acceptance first. Our data show that 81 percent of directs say yes to this request for delegation acceptance (assuming their managers have done MTO3s with them for six months). We don't need to share all the details in the vast majority of cases in order to get a yes.

One reason we do this is that a direct who has already agreed (81 percent of them) is much more likely to listen to the details *with an attitude of ownership and trying to solve the problem*. If we wait to ask until they've heard all the details, they will often listen to all the details in a defensive way, worrying about workload and priorities.

There's another reason to ask first before providing the details. If Sarah doesn't say yes immediately, she's likely to say something like, "Well, I could, but I'm worried about my workload" or "Well, yes, but I don't know how to do that."

In sales, this is what's called an objection. Salespeople love objections, because the objections give them clues as to what the person's concerns are. Their next line is, "If I can address your concerns, will you agree?" So, when you are delegating a task, you might say, "If I can sort out your workload, will you be able to do this work?" or "If I can teach you how, will you do it?" The person will either give you more concerns (in which case, you repeat this step) or will say yes. When they say yes, you now know how to make small changes as you walk through the details of what's involved to satisfy their concerns.

4. Describe the Task or Project in Detail

This turns out to be the easy part of delegation. Walk the direct through what the responsibility is in detail. Explain to them what they'll do at a reasonable level. Because this is something you yourself are doing now, you're an expert on how it's done. It typically starts with, "Here's what I do . . ."

"*Here's what I do* each month to write the monthly operations report. I get the raw data from the VP's admin on the 10th. I have until the 15th to turn in a 200-word report that describes what happened to our products in the marketplace. I sit down, and review what the plans were, and what the previous month's results were. Then I look at the detailed data and sketch a rough story of what I think occurred. I let that draft sit overnight. Then I come back and polish it. Usually, I then send it over to my peer, Mike, who has exposure to our markets. I ask him to make sure what I'm saying makes sense. Once he's agreed, I send it in an e-mail back to the VP's admin. It takes me about an hour to draft, and about 15 minutes to polish, every month."

5. Address Deadline, Quality, and Reporting Standards

Once you've gotten acceptance, and covered the details, it's time to cover three things that always get covered when work passes from one person to another: the deadline, the quality standard the work has to meet, and whatever reporting frequency is required.

You might say it like this: "You'll report on the 15th of each month, and here's the template. This is work that is seen by the VP, so it needs to be perfect. I want weekly updates, in our O3, with Red/Amber/Green status standards."

13

Common Questions and Resistance to Delegation

What Should You Delegate?

If you're still struggling to figure out what to delegate, there are four tasks you likely engage in currently as a manager that you could delegate to your directs (even, in some cases, rotating these responsibilities among them).

1. *Reporting.* Creating reports isn't an effective use of your time. The knowledge one gains from a report doesn't have to come through creating the report—just read it, after someone else creates it. The person who creates it will learn from doing it each week or month.
2. *Meetings.* Stop running your meetings. Have one of your directs be a facilitator, that is, responsible for working with the agenda and facilitating the meeting. This frees you up to contribute more and to pay even more attention to your directs.
3. *Presentations.* You're probably quite competent at presenting, but perhaps your staff isn't. If you are assigned a presentation,

delegate it to a direct, and help the direct create the slide deck (if necessary) and rehearse. The way you learn to do a thing is to do the thing.

4. *Projects*. Follow the same procedure as for presentations.

What If a Direct Repeatedly Says No to Delegation Requests?

A direct rejecting a delegation request is, of course, the danger of a model that is built on relationship power and persuasion rather than on role power and giving orders. Your directs can say no.

The risk of being told no, however, is worth it, and here's why. When you use your role power to get something done, you get what is known as "compliance energy" from your directs. They know they "have to." They'll do it, but they may not be excited about it. Just think about your friends who have worked for a top-down, dictatorial, no-relationships boss. It sapped their energy and effectiveness, didn't it?

When you use the persuasion built on trust from your relationship power to get something done, you get what is known as "commitment energy." The direct knows they can say no, *and they choose to say yes. That ability to choose frees up that last full measure of work devotion that we want from them.*

When They Say No, Honor It, Initially

We've covered in our previous guidelines the requirement to honor a no when you've asked your directs a question. Never ask a question whose answer you don't intend to honor.

This is best proved through the negative. If you ask one of your directs a question, you're implying that the direct's answer has merit, right? If she gives you the answer you "didn't want" and you say,

"Well, I don't think you understand what's going on here . . ." then you're essentially saying, "I expected you to say the right thing—what I wanted—and you should have known that the question was really window dressing, and now I am going to get what I wanted all along through the use of my role power."

If you start overruling answers to some of the questions you pose, you're going to have directs tell you what you want to hear even when it's false, wrong, or unethical. The trumping of honest answers leads to dishonesty. Period.

So, if a direct says no, you are obligated to accept the demurral. Usually, this means one of two things, tactically. Either you will ask another direct, which works far better than most managers expect, or you will do the work yourself. Strategically, of course, it also suggests that you look at your efforts toward building trusting relationships and asking yourself, "Did I not see something, or was I unaware of what her situation was?

The overwhelming majority of nos are based on workload issues. Sometimes directs are right—they have too much to do. But that's rarer than most understand. Most of us are surprisingly flexible when it comes to taking on more work. We can take on more than we think. *Eustress* sometimes has to become *distress* to know where the dividing line is.

After Two Demurrals, Examine Your Assumptions

The first time you're told no, accept it. There's nothing wrong with probing, however, and trying to overcome the objection. Then, honor the no and walk away.

If this happens a second time, do the same thing, at first. Probe. Try to overcome. Then, if the answer is still a no, step back before you ask someone else. Ask yourself, "What do I think his workload is? Is it close to being overwhelming? Is this no a part of a weakening of our relationship that has larger implications?" Look back over the past few weeks for clues to a change in your relationship, which might include any of the following:

- Behavior changes
- Change of tone in conversations
- Fewer e-mails
- Change of tone in e-mails
- Changes in schedule
- Changes in mood
- Changes in attendance
- Changes in meeting behaviors and interactions

A note here about a second demurral. It's not unusual for someone to say yes to several delegations in a row, and then to say no, followed by more yeses. If you then get another no, those two nos don't qualify as a pattern. (If they did, we'd be saying that a yes should be mandated all along.) What we're talking about in this guidance is the direct who says no repeatedly, as a pattern—someone who doesn't say yes.

After getting two demurrals, take time in a One On One to ask questions of the direct. Actually, you don't have to ask the questions during an O3; you just have to be ready to have a five-minute conversation, and it won't work to ask these questions right after the direct has said no. The direct will simply defend what she has already said rather than switching gears to analyze the situation. We're suggesting this to give you and your direct some time and space to reflect. The O3 is simply the natural place to ask the questions.

14

How to Start Delegating

DELEGATION IS THE EASIEST PART of the "Management Trinity" to roll out, because you can (almost) start delegating right away. We recommend that you build your relationships first, but you can move somewhat quickly.

There is one problem with delegating earlier in the rollout process than at the end of the process. If you delegate before you've rolled out feedback and coaching, you won't have those tools at your disposal if you need them in order to help the direct to whom you've delegated responsibilities.

If you've chosen to wait until after you've rolled out the other three tools, roll out delegation in the same way. Schedule some time in your staff meeting—30 minutes is fine. Walk them through the Delegation Model, just as you have done with the other models.

Explain that you're going to start slowly and that you will choose whom to delegate to based on what the direct is good at, likes, wants, and needs to do in terms of performance and goals. Remind them again that when you ask them to accept the delegation, it's okay to say no.

If you want to build the capabilities of your team, you don't need to send them to a lot of training sessions. Just ask them to step up by pushing some work down. Your best team members will relish the challenge.

Afterword

I'VE SHARED A LOT of detailed, actionable guidance here, to help you start using the Management Trinity. I've shared it because we know it works, and because it's teachable.

And, in all the details and recommendations, I hope I haven't obscured what the engine of your greatness as a manager can be:

Love.

If you want to be a great manager, do these things with love. What I mean is professional love: the willingness to risk yourself for the benefit of another. It means doing something that may be a little more difficult for you, as a way of showing respect for your colleagues and your organization.

You can be demanding while also showing respect for your team. You don't have to withhold positive feedback. You can give negative feedback with love in your heart. You can deliver tough messages with kindness. You don't have to be mean, short, or disrespectful to challenge people. You don't have to be brusque, or rude. You don't have to "act like the boss." Nor do you have to sugarcoat hard messages. Be direct, and be kind doing it. That takes love.

Today, part of why management isn't held up in a noble way is because nobody's been teaching us how. And it's also because we've gotten away from loving our colleagues and team members.

But it doesn't have to be that way. Choose the harder right, instead of the easier wrong. Love is the engine to help you get there.

To the long-standing members of the Manager Tools community, thank you for your support. Thank you for your hard work to become an ethical, professional, highly effective manager. Knowing that our friends, colleagues and clients have been eagerly listening— from when there were only 100 of us, that first week in 2005—has made the growth of Manager Tools a labor of love.

To those of you who put up with my rambling; to those of you who wrote to us asking that the podcasts be kept to 22 minutes because that was the length of your commute and your spouse didn't like you sitting in the car in the driveway finishing a podcast after you got home; to those of you who sent us gifts and wrote us hundreds of poignant thank-you notes and e-mails about podcasts that helped you through a rough time: it is still a great privilege and a joy to serve you.

To John Hoffman, thanks for being my first corporate client and a great friend, so many many years ago.

To Eldon Schaffer, thanks for persisting all those years ago when I told you no, no, no.

To Gerhard Gross, and Dan McGuire, and Dan West, and Trevor Woods, and Marc Grainger, and Charlie Cheng, and Craig Glidden, and Karen Adams, and Bruce Cakebread, and Rodney Woods, and Jon Basden, and Linda Gottschalk, and Richard Rothschild, and Adam Antoniewicz, and Gwynne Shotwell, and Matt Deluhery, and Lauren Dreyer, and Bill Reilly, and Dirk Van de Bunt, and John Brown, and Steve Holden, and Marc Strand, and Paula Manning, and Ken Finch, and Joe Franke, and Michael Keithley, and Joe Poux, and Ken Brown, and Thomas Cunningham, and Phil Radford, and Nate Richards, and Ryan Carson and Kirk Botula, and Rich Ruh: Thank you, my friends.

When I write our guidance, I think of you. Be worthy of your title: Manager.

Mark Horstman
Pebble Beach, CA
February 2006—March 2016

Index

Note: Page references in *italics* refer to figures.